THE
KEEN SHOT'S
MISCELLANY

THE
KEEN SHOT'S
MISCELLANY

by
PETER HOLT

Pelen Holt
2008

Quiller

Copyright © 2008 Peter Holt

First published in the UK in 2008
by Quiller, an imprint of Quiller Publishing Ltd

British Library Cataloguing-in-Publication Data
A catalogue record for this book
is available from the British Library

ISBN 978 1 84689 039 0

Printed in Malta by Gutenberg Press Ltd.

Quiller

An imprint of Quiller Publishing Ltd

Wykey House, Wykey, Shrewsbury, SY4 1JA
Tel: 01939 261616 Fax: 01939 261606
E-mail: info@quillerbooks.com
Website: www.countrybooksdirect.com

DEDICATION

*In memory of my father Vesey Holt
who loved anything to do
with shooting.*

ACKNOWLEDGEMENTS

The Author and Publishers are grateful to the
following for permission to reproduce
copyright material:

The BASC for permission to use assorted nuggets of advice; Farlows of Pall
Mall for use of an extract from their website; Robert Milner for permission to
reproduce extracts from his book *Retriever Training – A Back to Basics Approach*;
Witherby Publishing Ltd. for permission to use extracts from *Record Bags And
Shooting Records* by Hugh S. Gladstone, and also for an extract from *The Art
of Shooting And Rough Shoot Management* by Leslie Sprake; Swan Hill Press for
permission to reprint extracts from *The Small Shoot* by David Hudson, *Rough
Shooting* by Mike Swan, *Gamekeeping* by David Hudson, *Birds, Boots and
Barrels*, by Giles Catchpole and Bryn Parry and from *Complete Guide to Ferrets*
by James McKay; Rosie Whitaker for permission to reprint extracts from her
father Sir Joseph Nickerson's book *A Shooting Man's Creed* (Swan Hill Press);
Country Life for permission to reprint an extract from *Letters to Young
Sportsmen on Hunting, Angling and Shooting*, by Major Kenneth Dawson and
others; Piffa Schroder for permission to reprint an extract from *Fair Game - A
Lady's Guide to Shooting Etiquette*.

Every effort has been made to obtain
permission to reproduce extracts but in some
cases this has not been possible.

INTRODUCTION

I HAVE HAD TREMENDOUS FUN WRITING THIS BOOK. If I have achieved nothing else it has been a crash course in the whole business of shooting: history, anthology and current practice.

My favourite story concerns the early nineteenth century, blind-in-one-eye sculptor Sir Francis Chantrey whose miraculous shot of two woodcock with one barrel made him the toast of the smartest salons throughout the land. And I am indebted to my friend Keith Ashbourne for inviting me on yet another fine day at Ruckley where on a picker-up's van I spotted a bumper sticker with the sublime lament: 'So many cats, so few recipes.'

I have dedicated this book to my late father who spent much of his life shooting. He averaged forty days a season without difficulty, achieving around seventy-five on several golden years in the 1970s. (I have to admit to far fewer days than him.) I would have liked to have added a dedication to my wife Sarah but frankly it would have fallen on stony ground. A keen hunting person, an MFH indeed, she finds the idea of shooting faintly ridiculous. I retaliate by telling her that my idea of purgatory is the thought of spending six hours in the saddle *without lunch*.

And a shooting day is nothing without a decent lunch. Some might even argue that the shooting lunch is as important as the sport itself. As the Victorian shooting writer J. J. Manley observed: 'A full hour or an hour and a half devoted to luncheon is not time lost, to say nothing of the agreeable way of spending it.' How right he was. I am not one of those who enjoy a brief pause for a sausage in a bun, huddled in a drafty barn, seated on straw bales and surrounded by a tribe of wet spaniels trying to force their way onto my lap. How miserable is that! No, what is needed is a proper sit-down lunch, preferably at 1 pm and out again at 2.15 allowing for a couple of drives in the afternoon. Others prefer to shoot through so that they can get stuck into the booze until late. This is not to my taste. But whatever the case, lunch must be comfortable and somewhere warm.

Finally, while I have the stage, may I make a plea for greater safety in the shooting field. I have seen some dodgy shots during the 2007 season, not only from the numerous newcomers to shooting but from seasoned guns as well. One friend of mine got badly peppered in a grouse butt. Apparently some of the other guns were engaged in 'competitive shooting' to see how many birds they could shoot. Such larking about might seem amusing, but it goes well against the sporting spirit. Col. Peter Hawker would turn in his grave. And what is this nasty habit that novice guns have for holding their weapons so that they are pointing forward, directly at the beaters, rather in the manner of Dad's Army? This may be acceptable for clay pigeons. But it's scandalous when you're shooting game. When not actually firing his piece, a gun's barrels should be either upwards or downwards and nowhere in between. Do shooting schools these days teach nothing about safety?

I am sure I have omitted many shooting stories that seem obvious to readers. Please let me have them for Volume Two.

INVALUABLE ADVICE FOR THE START OF THE SEASON

THE GRANDFATHER OF SHOOTING, the great Victorian shot Lt. Col. Peter Hawker*, had strict words of advice regarding poor shooting. He wrote in his 1844 manual *Instructions To Young Sportsman*: 'One who vexes himself about missing a fair shot, is less likely to support himself at all times as a first-rate performer, because that vexation alone might be the very means of his missing other shots, and therefore he could not be so much depended on as another man, who bore the disappointment with good humour.' In other words, *never* give yourself a hard time if you miss a bird. Having shot like a twat, walk away from your peg with a grin and declare that you're having a great day.

✱ Hawker is regarded by many as England's greatest shot. Sir Ralph Payne-Gallwey, nineteenth century commentator, expert wildfowler and a superb shot himself, said of Hawker: 'In the style of the game shooting he pursued he has probably no equal; as a snipe shot he has never been, and perhaps never will be, equalled – fourteen to fifteen snipe without a miss in as many shots, and with a flint gun, speaks volumes as to his skill.' Hawker once killed seventy-seven partridges out of seventy-eight. His detailed diaries reveal that he became most irritable if a bird cost him more than one barrel.

DOG TERMS

A brace of pointers or setters (i.e. two)
A leash of pointers or setters (three)
A couple of spaniels (two)
A couple and a half of spaniels (three)

EARLY DAYS

The first record of a bird being shot in Britain appears in the household accounts of Hunstanton Hall, Norfolk, seat of the le Straunge family. In November 1533 we read of 'a watter hen kylled with the gun.' A later entry records an entry of 'item receyvd of Mathew the Smyth for a gone makyn… 2 shillings.'

Such behaviour did not go down well with Henry VIII and his parliament. A year after Henry's death in 1548 Parliament passed 'an acte against the shootinge of shot.' The use of firearms for shooting game did not take off properly in Britain until the end of the sixteenth century and still the authorities considered it an accursed sport.

Upon ascending the throne in 1603, James I remarked, 'Hunting with running hounds is the most honourable and noble sort of sport, but it is a thievish form of hunting to shoot with gunnes…'

Over in India, they thought entirely the opposite. The Moghul Emperor Akbar (1556 to 1605) loved shooting so much that he gave his weapons names. With a gun called 'Jitmall' he shot around four thousand birds and another named 'Sangram' claimed 1,019 animals. His successor, the Moghul Jehangir, kept what was possibly the world's first game book. In forty-seven years of shooting Jehangir killed 3,213 animals and 13,954 birds (mostly sitting.)

FLYING TARGETS

THE ITALIANS, GERMANS AND EVEN THE JAPANESE were shooting birds in the air as far back as 1500. But the art of shooting airborne targets didn't gain popularity in England until 150 years later. The social commentator Richard Blome declared in 1686, 'It is now the mode to shoot flying.'

By the end of the eighteenth century shooting was rapidly growing in popularity, but it must have been darned tricky shooting a rabbit with a flint lock, let alone a bird on the wing. Shooting writer Hugh S. Gladstone points out in his 1920s book *Record Bags and Shooting Records* that by 1800 the flint lock gun was considered to be almost perfect. 'We must pause for a moment to consider this false zenith of perfection,' writes Gladstone. 'Armed with this weapon, which must have taken considerable time and care to load, the sportsman would always be at the mercy of his flint. Damp, wind and other causes made its operations so uncertain that the phrase "a flash in the pan" has been handed down to us as a synonym for disappointment and we can picture a sportsman, during a shower, carefully holding the lock of his gun under his coat tail to avoid a certain missfire.'

Gladstone explains how shooting at moving objects must have been very different from that today. 'The injunction that the gun should be aligned, but always maintaining a swing corresponding with the velocity of the moving object aimed at and fired directly the butt of the gun makes contact with the shoulder, must have been impossible. To kill a crossing bird, at but twenty paces, our ancestors must have had to aim and maintain their swing for a considerable period so as to allow for the slow ignition and the interval that occurred between pulling the trigger and the charge leaving the muzzle of the gun.'

Gladstone concludes that with practice it would be possible to shoot most kinds of game respectably, with perhaps the exception of snipe.

Generally the early English sportsman had much to put up with. The British historian George Trevelyan pointed out that there was no luxury about the field sports of the eighteenth century. 'Hard exercise and Spartan habits were the condition of all pursuit of game. This devotion took the leaders of the English world out of doors, and helped to inspire the class that then set the mode in everything from poetry to pugilism, with an intimate love and knowledge of woodland, hedgerow and moor, and a strong preference for country over town life which is too seldom found in the leaders of fashion in any age or land.'

A SPICE OF CHIVALRY

One of the most notable nineteenth century American sporting writers was a Philadelphia physician called Elisha Jarrett Lewis, a fanatical shot who spent much of his time travelling across the States on hunting expeditions. Lewis had strong opinions on everything from the value of a good night's sleep before going shooting to the treatment of corns after a day's walking up. But he reserved particular scorn for people whose enjoyment of shooting was based on quantity rather than quality.

'Our Indians look upon this habit of the white man with the utmost horror,' he wrote in his 1857 book *The American Sportsman*. 'He kills and wastes, say they, without object; and riots over life as if it were a thing of no value. The game vanishes from his desolating path, and the ground is covered by his destroying hand with that which he does not mean to use.'

Lewis concluded, 'The sportsman should have a spice of chivalry in his composition. He should not be merely a wanton and reckless destroyer.'

BATS

While on his 1868 tour of Egypt, Edward VII, Prince of Wales, began a day's sport by bagging twenty-eight flamingos on the Nile at Luxor during the morning. That afternoon Eddie moved on to the tomb of the Pharaoh Ramses IV where he started on the bats. Bats fly at not much more than 35 mph – about the speed of a partridge – so they aren't too tricky. Alas, the Prince was not on form. He bagged only one.

✳ Down in Australia they love bat shooting. During the 1950s shotgun owners in Queensland were issued with free cartridges in order to cull fruit bats that were destroying crops. And over in New South Wales, the Clybucca and Kempsey District Bat Hunting Club would hold an annual moonlight fruit bat cull and midnight barbeque.

CHANGE

SYNDICATE SHOOTING began properly in the 1930s. Many of the big estates had been broken up after the First World War and sporting rights were now let to small shoots.

But not everybody approved of the new order in shooting. The country sports writer Julian Tennyson summed up this disturbing state of affairs in his 1938 book *Rough Shooting From Month To Month*: 'It is safe to say that no sport in England has undergone such changes during the last seventy years as has shooting. At the beginning of the century shooting was the rich man's monopoly; those who shot the land were the squire, the man with the hereditary country estate, and any other country gentleman whose means and instincts inclined him to it. But now their estates have been broken up and either divided among the tenant farmers or sold as separate plots.'

Tennyson lamented that this sad state of rural affairs had produced that newfangled shooting arrangement – the syndicate.

'The syndicate is made up of men "in the City". Seventy years ago they would not have been able to reach conveniently a shoot which was any distance from London. Nowadays, however, they can have the sporting rights over most or all of the landowner's estate, which can be reached by rail or road in a couple of hours. Thus the City dweller who once knew nothing and thought nothing of shooting, now has as much control over it as the countryman, or even more. And of course this means that shooting has lost something of its fine art. The new sportsman has neither the time nor the inclination to study it as it was studied in the old days; his keeper does the work, and he reaps the reward.'

Tennyson concluded with a bitchy flourish: 'The breaking up of estates has made shooting possible for the multitude. Anyone who has a second-hand gun and one hundred pounds to spare can take "a bit of shooting". To them shooting is no more than a weekend diversion and a novelty. They know nothing of the ways of partridge, pheasant or hare, nothing of the fascinations of keepering. They don't wish to. Such things don't interest them. They never see further than the end of their gun barrels.'

✳ Julian Tennyson was the great-grandson of Queen Victoria's Poet Laureate. He lived in Suffolk and was a regular contributor to *The Field* and *Country Life*. He was killed in Burma early in 1945.

RURAL MYTH

A story is told of the novice shot who failed to unload after a drive and whose gun subsequently went off while travelling in the shoot vehicle. 'My God,' he exclaimed to his shocked and deafened fellow guns, 'I'm terribly sorry about that…quite extraordinary…exactly the same thing happened to me last week…'

A LEGENDARY DRIVE

During the 1890s, Lord Leicester, host at Holkham Hall, Norfolk, arguably Britain's greatest Victorian shoot, was in the habit of giving his guests only one drive. Guns and beaters spent all morning pushing the pheasants into one place without a shot being fired. Then they had a brief spot of lunch before getting into position for the only drive of the day.

The guns lined up three deep before almost every bird on the estate was driven over them. It took great skill for the keepers to trickle the birds out so that they didn't flush. The bag could come to over one thousand head of pheasant and partridge.

Incidentally, lunch at Holkham was a miserable affair. Leicester expected his guests to swallow a sandwich while standing up in a field and talking was forbidden in case it disturbed the birds. Wives unwelcome.

ETHICS

America's National Rifle Association (NRA) Code of Ethics:

❧I will consider myself an invited guest of the landowner, seeking his permission, and so conducting myself that I may be welcome in the future.

❧I will obey the rules of safe gun handling and will courteously but firmly insist that others who hunt with me do the same.

❧I will obey all game laws and regulations, and will insist that my companions do likewise.

❧I will do my best to acquire those marksmanship and hunting skills, which insure clean, sportsmanlike kills.

❧I will support conservation efforts, which can assure good hunting for the future generations of Americans. I will pass along to younger hunters the attitudes and skills essential to a true outdoor sportsman.

...And the five 'golden rules' of *The Code of Good Shooting Practice* as laid down by the British Association of Shooting and Conservation (BASC):

❧The safe conduct of shooting must show respect for the countryside and consideration for others.

❧Shoot managers must endeavour to deliver enhancement of wildlife conservation, habitat and the countryside.

❧Reared gamebirds should be released before the start of their shooting seasons.

❧Respect for quarry is paramount. It is fundamental to mark and retrieve all birds. Shot game is food and must be treated as such.

❧Game management and shooting must at all times be conducted within the law and the principles of this Code of Practice.

Which do you prefer?
This could lead to hours of debate in the gun room...

HAWKER ON HIS DOGS

NINETEENTH CENTURY SHOOTING LEGEND Lt. Col. Peter Hawker held strong views on gundogs. For example, poodles were no good for retrieving duck from a punt as they were 'apt to be sea-sick.'

The Colonel was responsible for introducing the Labrador into England from its native Newfoundland, Canada, in the early 1800s. But he never seems to have found the perfect dog and spent much of the time complaining about canine companions.

After shooting forty-five partridges and one hare he noted in his diary entry of 1 September 1819: 'I have now to record one of the most brilliant day's shooting I ever made in my life, when I consider the many disadvantages I had to encounter. I had but three dogs: poor old Nero, who was lame when he started; Red Hector, who was so fat and out of wind that he would scarcely hunt; and young Blucher, a puppy that never was in a field but three times before, and who till this day had never seen a shot fired.'

AGED KEEPERS

The late great sportsman Lord Leverhulme had a rule that if the combined ages of the gamekeeper and his employer amounted to more than one hundred, then one of them had to go....

DOUBLE BARRELS

UNTIL THE END OF THE EIGHTEENTH CENTURY double barrelled guns were considered extremely unsporting. The English sportsman reckoned that if you couldn't kill something with one shot then you shouldn't shoot it in the first place. However, the Italians would have none of this nonsense and had been making twin barrelled weapons as far back as 1650.

By the early nineteenth century English gunmakers were producing a few double flint locks. But proper gentlemen scorned them. The 1831 obituary of John Hunt, a shooting man from Tottenham (of all places), praised him as 'so true a lover of fair play he would have scorned to use a double-barrel.'

HUMMING BIRDS

The entire collection of humming birds at London's Natural History Museum was shot by Lord Walsingham, a keen lepidopterist, who collected moths and butterflies from a young age. He dispatched the humming birds by peppering them with powder shot thereby causing as little damage as possible.

Walsingham, who donated his collection of over 260,000 specimens to the museum, was arguably the finest shot of his generation. On 30 August 1888, in an extraordinary display of selfishness and grandiosity, the peer went alone onto Blubberhouse Moor, Yorkshire, and single-handedly shot a record bag of 1,070 grouse.

The first drive began at 5.12 am and the last drive ended at nearly 7.30 pm after fourteen hours and eighteen minutes of shooting. 1,062 birds were brought in that night, twenty-two were picked the next day and twelve were found when shooting the same ground two days later.

Walsingham fired 1,550 cartridges in twenty drives. During one drive he killed three grouse in one shot. His average kill to cartridge ratio was over seventy per cent. So what was it like to have been the only gun on such a massive day? 'The one thing everybody says is "How tired you must have been, how your head and shoulder must have ached." I never had the semblance of a headache or bruise of any kind; nor was I in the slightest degree tired. I played cards the whole evening afterwards as usual.'

Walsingham was spurred on to achieve the record having been snubbed by Edward VII who had just turned down an invitation to shoot at Blubberhouse because he didn't think it would be a big enough day. Walsingham was determined to prove the king wrong.

Walsingham's love of shooting was his downfall. He spent so much on high living (as well as being robbed by unscrupulous agents) that he went spectacularly bankrupt just before the First World War. He spent the last years of his life abroad and died in 1919.

PEG NUMBERING

In most shoots throughout Britain, the pegs number from right to left. But the only county where this does not happen is Lincolnshire. Unkind folk say that this anomaly stems from the First World War when very few Lincolnshire men ended up in the trenches. Instead, they stayed on the land growing potatoes. Thus, with an absence of military training, they never learned to number from the right...

THE VERY BEST SHOT

THE REV. WILLIAM B. DANIELS, author of an early nineteenth century tract called *Rural Sports*, decreed that 'the real sportsman feels a twinge whenever he sees a hen pheasant destroyed.' Large bags were 'unsportsmanlike' and he said it was 'the exploit, rather than the abundance' that mattered. The Rev. Daniels had particular scorn for a Mr J. W. Coke who on a shoot in Norfolk on 7 October 1767, scored a record bag when he killed eighty partridges for ninety-three shots in eight hours. 'He is the very best shot in England,' Daniels grudgingly admitted, adding enviously, 'He is so capital a marksman that, as he inflicts death whenever he pulls the trigger, he should in mercy forbear such terrible examples of his skill.'

FOR CARRYING PARTY TO COVERT

In Victorian times the game cart caused as much discussion and oneupmanship between guns as a new Range Rover does today. The best game carts were produced by a Norfolk manufacturer called Alfred Palmer and Sons. They built four models:

❧ 'No. 1 Gentlemen's two-wheel game-cart, suitable for carrying party to covert, fitted with luncheon-box and coat-box. Interchangeable holders in single or double rows can be made to suspend upwards of 120 brace of birds; also hare rack with twenty-eight hooks; automatic ventilation and rack for five guns.'

❧ 'No. 2. Four-wheel game-van, similar to the above, but longer; will suspend upwards of two hundred brace of birds.'

❧ 'No. 3. Four-wheel game-truck, a cheaper vehicle for carrying about two hundred brace or upwards; not provided with the special fittings of the above, nor suitable for carrying gentlemen to covert. Can have, if required, a tarpaulin head. Has strong railed sides to admit air, and also to take transverse bars on which game can be suspended.'

❧ But the best shooting transport of all was the No. 4 - 'a van something like an omnibus, fitted with folding tables and other requisites for the purpose of serving the luncheon. There is also provision for guns and coats on inside, and for suspending some game on the outside.'

GLORIOUS STUFF

Mr William Scott Elliot of Arkleton, Dumfriesshire, who died aged ninety-one in 1901, set a record for having been out on the moors shooting grouse on seventy-four successive twelfths of August, from 1824 to 1898.

NEVER, NEVER...

A Father's Advice, the much-quoted shooting poem that begins with the words 'If a sportsman true you'd be…', was written not by an established writer but by a gifted amateur who composed the verses for his son who was learning to shoot. Old Etonian Mark Beaufoy (1854 to 1922) was Member of Parliament for Kennington and heir to a vinegar fortune. He ran the family factory in Battersea making everything from wine vinegar to mayonnaise. Beaufoy was a man with a social conscience and worked hard on behalf the London poor. Indeed, he helped in drafting the legislation that introduced the eight-hour working day. Away from London, he had an estate in Wiltshire and was a keen shooting man. It is for his verses that he is best known:

> If a sportsman true you'd be,
> Listen carefully to me
> Never, never let your gun
> Pointed be at anyone;
> That it may unloaded be
> Matters not the least to me.
>
> When a hedge or fence you cross,
> Though of time it cause a loss,
> From your gun the cartridge take
> For the greater safety sake.
>
> If 'twixt you and neighbouring gun
> Bird may fly or beast may run,
> Let this maxim e'er be thine:
> 'Follow not across the line.'
>
> Stops and beaters, oft unseen,
> Lurk behind some leafy screen;
> Calm and steady always be;
> 'Never shoot where you can't see.'
>
> Keep your place and silent be;
> Game can hear and game can see;
> Don't be greedy, better spared
> Is a pheasant than one shared.

You may kill or you may miss,
But at all times think of this —
'All the pheasants ever bred
Won't repay for one man dead.'

❋ More than 150 years earlier the eighteenth century author George Markland included a verse about dangerous shooting in his 1727 book *Pteryplegia, Or The Art Of Shooting Flying*. It has none of Beaufoy's punch but it is a fine cautionary tale that probably did the trick for a youth intent on abusing his muzzle loader:

A blooming youth, who had just passed the boy,
The father's only child and only joy,
As he intent designed the larks his prey,
Himself as sweet and innocent as they,
The fatal powder in the porch of death
Having in vain discharged its flash of breath,
The tender reasoner, curious to know
Whether the piece were really charged or no,
With mouth to mouth applied, began to blow.
A dreadful hiss! For now the silent bane
Had bored a passage thro' the whizzing train,
The shot all rent his skull, and dashed around his brain!
Unguarded swains! Oh! Still remember this,
And to your shoulder close constrain the piece,
For lurking seeds of death unheard may hiss.

THE WORLD'S BIGGEST BAG?

IT IS CALCULATED THAT THE BIGGEST BAG OF QUAIL – indeed probably the biggest bag of game ever recorded – was carried out circa 1580 BC by the Israelites in the Sinai desert. Exodus xii, 37, 38, states that the Children of Israel 'stood up all that day and all that night, and all the next day, and they gathered the quails: he that gathered least gathered ten homers.' A 'homer' has been estimated at around eighty gallons. On this basis it is assumed that the Israelites killed nine million quail in thirty-six hours. It is not surprising that what with all the decomposing innards of nine million quail, this feat was followed by a nasty outbreak of plague.

CATS

Ancient Egyptian tomb paintings show cats retrieving pheasant-like birds that have been killed with throw sticks. It is unknown whether anyone in England has ever trained their cat to retrieve a pheasant. Whatever the case, cat retrievers must be the stuff of keepers' nightmares.

BONEY BUM

Napoleon was a dangerous shot and once blasted the great military tactician Marshal Massena in the bottom. Bonaparte was not a gentleman on the shooting field and liked to blame others for his mistakes. Having shot Massena, he turned to the gun next to him, his long-suffering Chief of Staff Marshal Berthier, and asked, 'Why did you do that?'

Napoleon's enemy the Duke of Wellington was not much better. At various shoots he peppered Lord Granville, British ambassador to France, a beater and a washerwoman. Though quite what a washerwoman was doing in the shooting field is unknown.

FOR WHEN YOU TIRE OF PLAIN ROAST GROUSE

This recipe called *Grouse Supreme* works just as well with pheasant.

3 grouse, cleaned, soaked in salt water ½ hour, then rinsed. Remove shot.

½ cup flour

2 tablespoons dried parsley

2 tablespoons ground ginger

2 tablespoons paprika

1 tablespoon mustard powder

4 tablespoons walnut oil

4 tablespoons margarine or butter

½ cup honey

½ teaspoon ground black pepper

2 tablespoons Worcestershire sauce

¾ cup Madeira

Split birds in half. Season flour with one tablespoon each of parsley, ginger, paprika and mustard. Dry birds, roll in seasoned flour. Heat walnut oil and lightly brown each bird. Set aside. Pour remaining walnut oil into saucepan. Add butter and honey and melt over low heat. Add all other ingredients except for Madeira which you add after stirring for two minutes. Continue to stir near boiling point. Add seasoned flour to thicken. Put birds in baking dish, pour sauce over top. Bake at 350 degrees for twenty minutes. Reduce heat to 200 degrees for another twenty minutes. Remove, turn birds over and put back in oven for another ten minutes at 300 degrees or until brown.

POSH SPORT

The London districts of Pimlico and Belgravia were famous for their snipe bogs as late as 1820. The ninth Earl of Galloway regularly shot snipe on the site of the house he later inhabited at 85 Eaton Square, now one of London's smartest addresses.

THE GREAT BALLOON SHOOT OF '83

One of the more unusual quarries pursued in recent times was a hot air balloon shot by the late Richard Henry Piers Butler, seventeenth Viscount Mountgarret, as it passed above his Yorkshire grouse moor on an otherwise blissful shooting day in August 1983.

'What the hell do you think you're playing at?' roared the eccentric peer as the pilot skimmed the heather.

Red in the face with fury, Lord M took a pot shot. The shot found its mark and pellets struck the pilot in the neck.

This was to become one of the most celebrated shooting stories of the 1980s. Mountgarret appeared before the beak and was fined £1,100. Furthermore, he was banned from owning a shotgun. Apparently this inconvenience bothered him little. He continued to shoot by borrowing guns off friends.

CULTURAL GAP

A stroll through a book called *American Rough Shooting – The Practice and Pleasures of Sport Hunting* reveals the vast cultural gap that lies between the American and British sportsman.

Author Edward K. Roggenkamp III says that no hunter should be without an automatic pump gun. 'The advantage of an autoloader is its very rapid three or five-shot power package,' opines Roggenkamp, who includes a section on what action you should take if one of your party goes down with accidental gunshot wounds. 'Some hunters just do not feel comfortable without a magazine full of shells at the ready. Of course, when hunting woodcock, a migratory bird, the magazine must be plugged to hold only three shells. But many hunters place high value on the five-shot magazine when hunting slow-rising coveys or when shooting at fast-crossing pheasants.' Just the thing for those high Devon birds.

HOGZILLA

THERE WAS MUCH CHATTER in the American hunting world in 2007 concerning eleven-year-old Jamison Stone who used a pistol to kill what may have been the world's biggest wild boar. Quite what an eleven-year-old was doing with a .50 calibre Smith and Wesson revolver is mind-boggling. But whatever the case Jamison Stone's hog gained him instant stardom in the boonies.

The feral pig weighed 1,051 lb and measured 9 ft 4 in from snout to tail. We're talking hams as big as car tyres. Or seven hundred pounds of sausages.

Jamison, who killed his first deer aged five, was hunting with his father Mike in east Alabama. They tracked the animal for three hours before Jamison shot it eight times with his revolver. He finished it off with a point-blank head shot, his father standing by with a rifle in case the beast decided on a last gasp charge.

With Hogzilla finally dead in a creek bed, trees had to be cut down before he could be dragged out of the woods.

'It felt really good,' Jamison said. 'I probably won't ever kill anything else that big.' He added that he preferred shooting pheasants because they were 'less dangerous.'

Not all America was impressed. A website, monsterpig.com, set up by Stone Snr. to celebrate his son's achievement, attracted waves of hate mail.

As is usual on American blog spots, reasoned argument and high literary standards were not in evidence. Jamison was forced to read gems such as, 'hurry up enlist in the Army, I want to see you chased and shot at and maybe beheaded on video' and 'fucking fat redneck, I hope the boar babies come back and eat you.'

The rotund Jamison who looked like he had spent rather too long in the cookie jar, was also told 'I have to congratulate you because I didn't think it was possible for an eleven-year-old as large as yourself to chase a pig for three hours in hilly terrain. Incidentally, which one is the pig?'

BAD BUNNIES

RABBITS are estimated to cause more than £100 million worth of damage to crops each year in the United Kingdom. A single rabbit reduces winter wheat yields by an astonishing one per cent. But properly netted fields can reduce rabbit numbers on crops by up to ninety per cent. The UK rabbit population is now reckoned to be over forty million. The word bunny comes from the Gaelic *bun*, meaning rabbit.

THE SECRET OF LONGEVITY

'Many a brain-worker from the Senate, the Bar, and other callings,
many a harassed "City Man" , and many an idler for the
greater part of the twelve months, adds years to
his life by the wholesome work and unique
excitement of grouse shooting.'

Quote by Victorian sporting writer
J. J. Manley in 1880

BRITAIN'S RECORD BAG

THE ALL TIME RECORD BAG FOR A SHOOT IN BRITAIN was on 18 December 1913 at Hall Barn, Beaconsfield. The seven guns, including the Prince of Wales, later George V, shot 3,937 pheasants, three partridges, four rabbits and one various – a total of 3,945 head. However, this remarkable slaughter was dwarfed by a shoot in north-west Hungary four years earlier. On 10 December 1909, eight guns shooting on Count Louis Kariolyi's estate at Totmegyer, killed 6,125 pheasants, fifty partridges and 150 hares.

ECONOMICAL SHOOTING

PRINCE FREDERICK, DUKE OF YORK, was Commander in Chief of the British Army whose lacklustre performance in the unsuccessful Flanders campaign (1793 to 1798) during the French Revolutionary Wars earned him nursery rhyme immortality as the "Grand Old Duke of York.'

These shortcomings apart, Fred was a damned good shot. His great sporting moment happened on a shoot in Cambridgeshire in 1826 when he killed three pheasants with one barrel.

OVERKILL

God knows what Americans put their gun dogs through, but it must be rough. A US firm called Ready Dog has come up with a Gun Dog First Aid Kit that they say is essential for sportsmen heading off into the American wilderness. Included is the sort of stuff that could give your vet the jitters: stainless steel paramedic shears, forceps, skin stapler, hydrogen peroxide, aspirin, antihistamine, thermal emergency blanket, tourniquet, trauma dressing, eye wash, cold compress, rectal thermometer. And all this for a dog.

❋ When a reader of the *Shooting Times* enquired as to the best method of curing a spaniel of fatigue, the professional response was that the one essential dog 'medicine' a Gun should take shooting was a Mars Bar. The glucose in a Mars Bar delivers a quick energy boost and can prevent hypoglycemia caused by an excessive amount of energy let off in the field. But beware – too much chocolate can harm a dog.

POOR BUSTARD

We do not know the record British bag for the great bustard, long extinct, but in 1808 a man called Agars shot eleven in 'one' shot while out on the Yorkshire wolds. This suggests that the bustard was easy prey. Coupled with the fact that the bustard was exposed to a longer shooting season than other game birds – 1 September to 1 March – this perhaps explains why there are none left.

BEAT THIS

S UCH WAS THE QUANTITY OF PHEASANTS reared by the late Victorians, the second Marquis of Ripon managed to shoot 556,813 head of game in fifty-six years of shooting. He eventually dropped dead, gun in hand, on Dallowgill moor, Yorkshire, on 22 September 1923. He was seventy-one.

Ripon was the most flamboyant Victorian shot of them all. On a good day with the best loaders, he could have three guns blazing in succession, allowing him to kill twenty-eight pheasants a minute, with up to seven birds falling out of the sky at the same time.

It is often said that Ripon dropped dead in a grouse butt. Not so. Visitors to Dallowgill are perplexed to find the cairn marking the place of his final expiration actually fifty feet in front of the butts. The story goes that the drive having finished, Ripon stormed out of his butt and set off towards the keeper to whom he was going to deliver a bollocking for a terrible drive. He collapsed and died before he could get to the unfortunate underling. What makes this story rather unfathomable and tells one much about Ripon's obsession for big bags, is that he had just shot fifty-one grouse and one snipe to his own gun.

✻ Lord Ripon used to say that for a bird on the left the left foot needs to be moved to the left and then the right should be placed in front of it. Do the reverse for a bird on the right. Feet should not be too far apart.

———

✻ Between 1802 and 1853, when very few birds were reared, the doyen of early Victorian shooting Lt. Col. Peter Hawker bagged a mere 575 pheasants (out of a total of 17,753 game and wildfowl) in his lifetime. The question is: did Hawker have as much fun as Ripon? The answer is almost certainly yes.

WILD BILL WHITELAW

One of the most gossiped about shooting accidents of recent times happened in 1984 when Willie, Viscount Whitelaw, then Deputy Prime Minister and leader of the House of Lords, peppered his host, the seed magnate Sir Joseph Nickerson.

The incident happened on Britain's finest grouse moor, Wemmergill, in Teesdale, County Durham, where Sir Joseph held the shooting rights. It's not entirely clear what happened but it sounds like a gun shooting after his sell-by date. Whatever the case, Willie, sixty-six, tripped while holding his loaded Holland. Sir Joseph took one in the arm and his loader, a Mr Lindsay Waddell, received a nasty leg wound.

Sir Joseph was rushed to hospital where doctors were horrified to find lead shot deep in his stomach. Sir Joseph reassured them that this had come not from his friend's gun but rather from an excellent grouse upon which he had dined the night before...

✳ There was a tradition a century ago whereby if a gun wounded somebody in the shooting field he would donate his guns to the victim – not a bad consolation prize if they happened to be Hollands or Purdeys – and then leave the field never to shoot again. The police would not be bothered and no more would be said. Sadly, this is no longer the case. These days there are too many instances of people continuing to shoot even after they have peppered a beater or fellow gun.

RIGHT AND LEFT

THE PARTY TRICK OF LUIS I, King of Portugal (1838 to 1889) was to shoot pheasants alternately from each shoulder. A loader would stand each side of him passing him his guns which he would fire from both his right and left shoulders. Such a feat is almost unique in the history of shooting and his method was much admired at Sandringham during the 1880s where he was a frequent guest of the Prince of Wales. By using this extraordinary technique Luis could shoot up to two hundred pheasants in half an hour.

AHEM

THE WORLD'S LARGEST RECORDED BAG OF GAME ever achieved in a day was by Prince Alois of Liechtenstein and eleven chums on an October day in Austria in 1797. During fourteen hours of shooting the party claim to have shot 39,000 head, mainly hares and partridges. This works out at nearly four head per minute per gun. One doesn't like to question the honour of the House of Liechtenstein but, bearing in mind that the weapons would have been flintlocks, one has to think that someone was telling porkies.

THE LONGEST SHOOT ON RECORD is a 'chasse' in Bohemia that lasted twenty days. The twenty-three guns, including the Emperor of Austria and his wife Princess Charlotte, fired no less than 116,231 shots for 47,950 head (two killed for every five shots) that included stags, roe deer, wild boars, foxes, hares (an astonishing 18,273), pheasants, partridges, larks and quails. There were also fifty-four head of 'other birds' made up of blackbirds and thrushes.

THE BIRD CATCHER, THE PARTRIDGE, AND THE COCK

A bird catcher was about to sit down to a dinner of nothing but herbs when a friend unexpectedly arrived expecting a good meal. Since the bird catcher had caught nothing all day he decided to kill his tame decoy partridge. The partridge was most put out and pleaded for his life: 'What would you do without me when next you spread your nets? Who would chirp you to sleep, or call for you the covey of answering birds?' The bird catcher relented and spared his life. Instead, he picked a fine young cockerel. But the cock protested: 'If you kill me, who will announce to you the appearance of the dawn? Who will wake you to your daily tasks or tell you when it is time to visit the bird-trap in the morning?' The bird catcher replied, 'What you say is true. You are a capital bird at telling the time of day. But my friend and I must have our dinner.'

MORAL OF THE STORY: NECESSITY KNOWS NO LAW.

Aesop's Fable, circa 600 BC

FEW SHOTS

'An experienced sportsman may be compared with an experienced lawyer; the one is a man of few shots, but they always hit; the other of a few words, but they are always to the point.'

From The Dead Shot, *by 'Marksman', 1860*

THE TYPICALLY BRITISH PARTRIDGE

THE SHOOT WRITER LESLIE SPRAKE, who contributed to *Country Life* in the 1920s under the splendid pseudonym 'Middle Wallop', held firm views on what it was to be British. Here he explains why we should salute the partridge:

> I would suggest that when there is a reaction to the present 'Divorce Court Era', and the nation reverts to those dull but respectable characteristics known to the foreigner as 'stolid British virtues', it would be appropriate if the figure of a partridge were added to our national emblem – to typify fidelity! For this bird demonstrates all those qualities that should endear it to the family man – or woman. Thus we know that a partridge is faithful to its mate; the family circle is maintained until the children start their own 'establishments'; the parents are bold and self-sacrificing on behalf of their young; and last but not least they display that typically British virtue of attachment to locality (jealous foreigners term it insularity!) – the covey restricts its movements to a limited area which is no doubt considered to be greatly superior to any 'foreign' district.

From The Art of Shooting And Rough Shoot Management, *by Leslie Sprake, 1930*

IMPORTANT MOMENTS IN SHOTGUN DEVELOPMENT

❧ 1787. Henry Nock invents his patent breech for muzzle loaders. Nock positions the touch hole in the centre of the breech plug rather than on the side of the barrel. This means that the flash ignites the centre of the main powder charge giving a more rapid burn and increasing the velocity of the shot. With Nock's invention the very long barrels of the day are obsolete. Nock reduces barrel length to thirty inches thus reducing weight and producing a better balanced weapon. The increased power means that guns are now better for wing shooting rather than the shooting sitting of the past. Henry Nock's son-in-law is called James Wilkinson. Under Wilkinson's direction Nock's firm starts producing Army bayonets. In later years the company is to be renamed Wilkinson Sword.

❧ 1807. A shooting-mad Scottish Presbyterian minister, the Rev. Alexander John Forsyth, patents the first percussion cap igniting system, wedding priming powders to the ignition of firearms, therefore making the flint obsolete. Napoleon offers Forsyth £20,000 for his secrets, but Forsyth tells Boney where to stick his money. Forsyth later receives a pension for his loyalty from a grateful British government.

❧ 1829. Clement Pottet of France takes out a patent on a self-contained cartridge. This has a removable base incorporating a pocket for a priming compound whereby a percussion cap can be placed over a central nipple.

1836. Another Frenchman, Casimir LeFaucheux, patents his pinfire system.

1846. Paris gunsmith Bernard Houllier has an idea for a base wad which expands when fired. It overcomes one of the principal deficiencies of early breechloaders – gas leakage at the breech.

1850. LeFaucheux combines the Houllier wad with his pinfire concept and creates the first truly successful sporting shotgun cartridge. More significantly he also produces a breechloading shotgun with a drop down barrel to go with his cartridge. This is launched at London's Great Exhibition in 1851. The idea is copied by London gunmaker Joseph Lang. Other gunmakers including James Purdey, jump on the breechloading bandwagon, each making his own improvements.

1858. The big drawback of drop down barrels is closing the action. But this is rectified by Westley Richards of Birmingham who invent the first snap action closing mechanism.

1875. Birmingham wins again when Anson and Deeley produce the first hammerless shotgun, thus bringing shooting into a new era.

JOKE

A women is out shooting in the wilds of America when she comes across a male hunter walking towards her. The lady notices that the man has a compass hanging from his belt.

'What's the compass for?' she asks.

'It's to make sure I don't get lost when it gets dark,' he says, adding, 'Don't you every worry about getting lost?'

'Oh, I don't need to worry about that,' she says. 'If I get lost all I have to do is fire a shot into the air. Then all these men appear from behind every tree saying, "You're shooting behind it! You need to give it more lead!" It works every time.'

HOLLYWOOD

THE ONLY HOLLYWOOD STAR to appear engraved on a shotgun is Tom Hanks. A profile of Hanks sitting on a bench was etched onto the underside of a side-by-side 12-bore commissioned by movie director Robert Zemeckis to celebrate the film *Forest Gump*. The gun was made by Italian gun maker Ivo Fabbri who numbers many Hollywood celebrities among his clientele. Director Steven Spielberg owns a Fabbri over-and-under engraved with dinosaurs which he commissioned as a memento of his movie *The Lost World*.

PLAIN GERMAN

'GERMAN WOMEN OUT SHOOTING are almost always plain, and almost always widows. This is quite simply explained by the fact that in Germany, instead of standing waiting for nice high birds to be driven over the line as usually happens elsewhere, it is deemed more exciting for the guns to face each other from either end of, say, a belt of corn or barley and then to advance slowly towards each other, firing when anything appears. This is the famous Blucher manoeuvre, of "line faces line."'

From Fair Game – A Lady's Guide to Shooting Etiquette, *by Piffa Schroder, Ashford, Buchan and Enright, 1988*

ROUGH TYPES

In his book *Rough Shooting*, Dorset shooting expert Mike Swan gives this vital piece of advice for guns: 'Beware of using camouflage clothing to excess. In today's social climate members of the public will be deeply suspicious of armed and military looking people. If you can get away with using a battered tweed jacket rather than army camouflage gear you will be more likely to be taken for a sportsman rather than a terrorist…'

From Rough Shooting, *by Mike Swan, Swan Hill Press, 1991*

PHEASANT DITTY

'Should pheasant rise, be most particular
He rises nearly perpendicular;
Wait a few seconds till your sight
Perceives his horizontal flight.'

Anon, early 19th century

GIN 'N JEFFREYS

Malcolm Lyell, flamboyant managing director of Westley Richards and later Holland and Holland in the 1950s and 60s, was known for his unorthodox business methods. While at Westley Richards, he managed to take over the highly respected, but old fashioned gunmakers W. Jeffrey.

'Jeffrey was a fairly easy purchase,' Lyell recalled. 'The deal was agreed with Mr F. J. Pearce, the chairman, who was retired and lived in the country. He came up for the day…and met me for lunch at the Westbury Hotel. I'd warned Albert their barman to provide Mr Pearce with particularly potent dry martinis, which fortunately Mr Pearce accepted. By about 3 pm Mr Pearce agreed to the deal. Our accountant always says that the Jeffrey shareholders' fate rested upon those dry martinis and the fact that Mr Pearce had to catch a 4 pm train at Paddington in order to get home to Devon in time to feed his cats.'

Taken from The Shooting Field with Holland and Holland, *by Peter King*

DON'T SPARE THE RAMROD

A good reason for preferring breechloaders to muzzleloaders was given by an anonymous schoolboy in the first half of the nineteenth century. 'If a gun ain't got no ramrod,' the youngster explained, 'Your father can't lay one across your back when he ain't please with you out shooting…'

DUCHESS OF BEDFORD

THE GREATEST LADY SHOT OF THE EDWARDIAN ERA was Mary, Duchess of Bedford, amateur pilot of great renown, keen ornithologist and general all round country lady.

The game books at Woburn Abbey reveal that Mary's best average for one season was 2,392 head for 4,861 cartridges. She once killed 115 partridges to her gun in one day and her best average at driven grouse was sixty-seven for ninety-six cartridges. On 31 January 1928, armed with a 16-bore, she shot 273 'remarkably tall' pheasants and two jays for 366 cartridges.

Mary's love of shooting helps to explain the terrible tinnitus she suffered. In 1937, aged seventy-one and virtually deaf, the Duchess took off from Woburn in a Gipsy Moth which later crashed into the North Sea. Her body was never found.

WOODCOCK TRIVIA

The expression 'a feather in his cap' derives from the practice of sportsmen putting the pin feather of a woodcock he has shot in his cap band. The tiny feathers have also been much sought after by artists who paint miniatures.

A BIT OF A BORE

The most obscure gun ever produced was Cogswell and Harrison's 14 ¾ bore that made a brief appearance in the 1890s. The idea was that it would have similar size barrels as a 12-bore but they would be stronger, thus increasing resistance to dents. The makers claimed that it handled better than a 12-bore. A few of these strange weapons were made, as were the cartridges, but they never caught on.

ENSANGUIN'D

One of the first rants against field sports was penned by Henry Pye (1745 to 1813), who has been described as Britain's dullest Poet Laureate.

Pye's 1790 poem *Amusement* was a satire on the decadence of the age. Pye deplored the degeneracy of modern shooting and believed that far too much was being shot in the name of sport:

> Swoln opulence is not content to stray
> In anxious search through many a tedious day,
> Where constant hopes the eager thought employ,
> And expectation doubles every job:
> But the wing'd tribe, by care domestic bred,
> Watch'd with attention, with attention fed,
> Where'er the sportsman treads in clouds arise,
> Prevent his wish, and sate his dazzled eyes;
> And each redoubled shot with certain aim
> Covers the ensanguin'd field with home-bred game –
> Transporting joy! To vulgar breasts unknown,
> Save to the poulterer and the cook alone;
> Who search the crowded coop with equal skill
> As sure to find, almost as sure to kill.

The elevation of Pye to Poet Laureate in 1790 was greeted with astonishment by his contemporaries who regarded him as a useless poet with scant command of the English language. He produced some atrocious birthday odes, and his successor Robert Southey remarked during a moment of literary barrenness, 'I have been rhyming as doggedly and dully as if my name had been Henry James Pye.'

Strangely enough, Pye seems to have had a change of heart in the years after writing this poem. In 1807 he edited the fifth edition of the *Sportsman's Dictionary*, which was specifically aimed at shooting folk.

TED NUGENT

The world's greatest celebrity supporter of field sports is the American hard rock guitarist Ted Nugent, the man who once said: 'My idea of fast food is a mallard.'

Nugent's views on shooting everything from pheasants to paedophiles make the Countryside Alliance look like a bunch of nancies. 'Animal rights extremists are on record threatening to kill my children on the way to school because we eat pheasant,' says Nugent, 'Anyone who thinks hunting is terrible can kiss my ass.'

Nugent has sold thirty-five million albums worldwide and is the author of the best selling book *Kill It And Grill It* (2002). At the National Rifle Association's 2005 convention he received a standing ovation after he told delegates, 'I want carjackers dead. I want rapists dead. I want burglars dead. I want child molesters dead. I want the bad guys dead. No court case. No parole. Get a gun and when they attack you, shoot 'em.'

President George Bush loves Nugent. But Nugent thinks the president is wuss. Asked about Iraq, Nugent says, 'Our failure has been not to Nagasaki them.'

Other Nugent gems:

Feminists: 'What's a feminist anyways? A fat pig who doesn't get it often enough?'

Vegetarians: 'Vegetarians are cool. All I eat are vegetarians – except for the occasional mountain lion steak.'

Nugent is passionate about field sports. Away from the rock and roll circuit he spends much of his time at his Michigan ranch wildfowling, trapping and fishing. He has hosted TV reality shows where contestants have to kill their own food to survive. 'I feel that my sacred temple deserves the greatest fuel in the world and there's not only no better health food than venison and turkey and wildfowl.'

GOOD DAY, BAD DAY

'I can generally tell what sort of a day is in prospect when I shake hands with the keeper. A calloused hand, good day. Soft hand, poor day. This I find is a sure indication'.

From A Shooting Man's Creed, *by The late Sir Joseph Nickerson*

THE ROSE OF TEXAS

Most non-politically correct book of recent times is a splendid little manual titled *The Perfect Shot*. Author Kevin 'Doctari' Robertson, a Zimbabwean professional hunter and, wildlife vet, has assembled a series of photographs of wild animals with diagrams showing where best to place a shot for a clean kill.

Robertson has advice for whacking everything from zebras and warthogs to crocodiles and leopards. He says that 'correct first shot placement' is vital for successful sport hunting. A thorough knowledge of the 'vital for immediate life' organs (heart, lungs, brain and spinal column) from all angles is vital. Thus we learn that the best place to shoot a giraffe is in the brain ('surprisingly small', says Robertson).

Hippopotamuses are best dispatched by a shot to the heart or spine. But make sure the first shot kills your hippo. 'They kill more African natives than all other dangerous game animals put together,' Robertson points out. Meanwhile, the rhinoceros is best tackled with a high heart/lung shot. But rhino skin is incredibly thick so 'only the very best-quality solid bullets should be used.'

Robertson's most unusual advice concerns the buffalo which can be taken from behind with a shot up the anus. This is known as a 'Texas heart shot.'

WHY?

'If rabbits weren't so short behind
How many brilliant shots we'd find.

How many would succeed who fail
If pheasants hadn't so much tail.

If driven grouse would wait a bit,
Or woodcock less obscurely flit.

If snipe – but why go on like this?
We know it well who shoot and miss.'

Anon

JOHN SPEKE

One of the most famous shooting accidents concerns John Hanning Speke, the nineteenth century explorer who discovered the source of the Nile, great geographical mystery of the age.

Speke was a Victorian celebrity who combined astonishing feats of bravery with a healthy dose of controversy. His triumphant return to Britain from Africa was quickly trumped by fellow explorer and erstwhile friend (and some say lover) Richard Burton who claimed that he had in fact found the Nile's source. Burton claimed that the Nile began at Lake Tanganyika. Speke argued that the great river's journey actually began further into Africa at Lake Victoria.

As it turned out, Speke was correct, but that did not stop a vicious war of words between the two rivals. This was compounded after Speke returned home a national hero and within days Burton was all but forgotten.

Burton claimed that he could prove scientifically that Tanganyika was the source of the Nile and he was determined to meet Speke head on. Speke reluctantly agreed to meet his foe on stage in a public debate in Bath organised by the British Association for the Advancement of Science.

Speke may have been a flamboyant swashbuckler to his fans, but years of living on the edge had turned him into a nervous wreck in private. He hated public speaking and he knew that his wild image – he had a tendency to dress in native garb while on his travels which was considered simply not done, old boy – would be no match for Burton's cool scientific approach. On the day of the debate, to escape the bitching, Speke spent the day partridge shooting at his brother's estate at Box, outside Bath. While clambering over a stone wall he laid down his flintlock at half cock. Drawing the weapon towards him by the muzzle, one barrel exploded into his chest. He was dead within minutes. At least that is the official story.

That evening the conference hall in Bath was packed in anticipation of a good row. Sir Roderick Murchison, the master of ceremonies and Britain's top geographer, climbed the stage and announced that Speke had been killed while partridge shooting. The stunned audience listened instead to Burton reading a paper on the African kingdom of Dahomey 'in a voice that trembled.' Afterwards Burton 'wept long and bitterly' for his old friend.

Speke was buried in the church of Dowlish Wake, Somerset, at a small family funeral attended by the explorer David Livingstone. The inquest's official verdict was that Speke's death was accidental, and that his gun had gone off while he was lifting it over a wall. But most believed that he had shot himself. A granite obelisk to his memory was erected by public subscription in London's Kensington Gardens.

✳ It is very possible that Speke shot himself accidentally. There were many such accidents in Victorian times because of the practice of keeping your hammer gun fully-cocked when walking up game in case a bird suddenly got up. Loaders were taught to handle fully-cocked hammer guns at great speed as a matter of course. Even with the introduction of the breechloader in the mid-nineteenth century, Guns would put the safety catch to 'off' the moment they took to the field.

The modern practice of putting the safety catch forward only when you raise your gun to shoot was unknown in Victorian times, and even considered rather sissy. Legendary shot Archibald James Stuart Wortley, writing in the *Fur, Feather and Fin Series*, 1894, said that a grouse moor novice was often encouraged to shoot at stray grouse as he approached the butts before the first drive and to 'be ready with his gun' when picking up wounded grouse after a drive. Do that today and you'd never get another invitation.

✳ As well as writing about shooting, Archibald James Stuart Wortley was a much-admired portrait painter. His picture of the cricketer W. G. Grace hangs in the National Portrait Gallery. (He was also responsible for a rather dour portrait of the author's great great grandmother Anna-Maria Cludde!) Other works include a series of pheasant drawings that appear alongside sketches by famed sporting artist Archibald Thorburn in a 1895 book titled *The Pheasant*.

Stuart Wortley came from a landowning Yorkshire family and owned a seat called Wortley Hall (now a country house hotel) near Pontefract, Yorkshire. He was an exceptionally fine shot and was up there with Walsingham, Ripon and Duleep Singh.

SHOW OFF

Emperor Maximilian of Austria (1459 to 1519) is said to have killed one hundred wild duck with 104 shots…from a cross bow.

ANONYMOUS YARN

A donkey had to be put down so a grave was dug. The donkey was led to it and shot. The noise of the gun frightened a pigeon from the tree above the grave. The man who had just dispatched the donkey killed the pigeon with his second barrel.

THE MOUSE THAT NEARLY ROARED

AMERICAN SHOOTING COACH AND AUTHOR PETER BLAKELEY emphasises the importance of checking your barrels for blockages: 'I once had a client who almost loaded and fired his favourite side-by-side at the start of a lesson, but luckily discovered an obstruction just in time…an unfortunate mouse had crawled up there during the closed season, become lodged, and subsequently died. Firing the gun would have had disastrous results.'

THE EARL OF LONSDALE

The Kaiser was a frequent shooting guest of the fifth Earl of Lonsdale on his Cumbria grouse moor before the First World War. When taunted later about this, Lonsdale would reply, 'It only shows how careful one should be about picking up acquaintances when abroad.' Lonsdale, who gave boxing the Lonsdale Belt, was known in his time as 'England's Greatest Sporting Gentleman.' During the 1930s he was chairman of Arsenal Football Club.

SHOOT LEGEND NORMAN CLARKE

There are some good stories about Norman Clarke, instructor at Holland and Holland's North London shooting school during the 1960s.

Clarke was giving a lesson to a gentleman who was new to shooting. The man picked up his gun but failed to break it to check if it was loaded. Clarke gently ticked him off.

'But it's my gun and I know it's not loaded,' the man said.

'You could be wrong,' Clarke said.

'No,' the man protested. 'I know. And I'll bet you a million pounds that it isn't loaded.'

Clarke replied, 'And I will bet you that you won't put the barrels of the gun in your mouth and pull both triggers.'

His student did not take up the bet.

Another time, Clarke was giving a lesson to a know-all. Clarke tried to tell his student why he was missing the clays. The man snapped, 'I do not want to be interfered with while I am shooting.'

Clarke stood there saying nothing. Eventually the know-all sneered, 'Well, okay, go on then, show me what you can teach me.'

Clarke took the man's gun from him and said, 'Sometimes a shot has only a left hand so I shoot like this.' He shouted 'pull!' Lifting the gun with one hand he shattered a clay.

'Sometimes a shot has only a right hand.' He transferred the gun to his right hand and shot another clay.

'Sometimes they haven't any strength in either arm.' And he demolished a clay from the hip.

Finally, he added, 'Sometimes they can only shoot with the gun upside down.' And holding the gun upside down he finished off another clay.

The know-all apologised.

ANNOYING

'Nothing is more annoying – at least to us, and no doubt
generally to our friends – than to toil after game
all day and then have it totally ruined by the
ignorance of the cook.'

From The American Sportsman, *by Elisha Lewis, Philadelphia, 1857*

MR PICKWICK GOES ROOK SHOOTING

'THIS IS THE PLACE,' said Mr Wardle, pausing after a few minutes walking, in an avenue of trees. The information was unnecessary; for the incessant cawing of the unconscious rooks sufficiently indicated their whereabouts.

The old gentleman laid one gun on the ground, and loaded the other.

'Here they are,' said Mr Pickwick; and, as he spoke, the forms of Mr Tupman, Mr Snodgrass, and Mr Winkle appeared in the distance.

'Come along,' shouted the old gentleman, addressing Mr Winkle; 'A keen hand like you ought to have been up long ago, even to such poor work as this.' Mr Winkle responded with a forced smile, and took up the spare gun with an expression of countenance which a metaphysical rook, impressed with a foreboding of his approaching death by violence, may be supposed to assume. It might have been keenness, but it looked remarkably like misery. The old gentleman nodded; and two ragged boys commenced climbing up two of the trees.

'What are these lads for?' inquired Mr Pickwick abruptly. He was rather alarmed; for he was not quite certain but that the distress of the agricultural interest, about which he had often heard a great deal, might have compelled the small boys attached to the soil to earn a precarious and hazardous subsistence by making marks of themselves for inexperienced sportsmen.

'Only to start the game,' replied Mr Wardle, laughing.

'To what?' inquired Mr Pickwick.

'Why, in plain English, to frighten the rooks.'

'Oh, is that all?'

'You are satisfied?'

'Quite.'

'Very well. Shall I begin?'

'If you please' said Mr Winkle, glad of any respite.

'Stand aside, then. Now for it.'

The boy shouted, and shook a branch with a nest on it. Half a dozen young rooks in violent conversation, flew out to ask what the matter was. The old gentleman fired by way of reply. Down fell one bird, and off flew the others.

'Take him up, Joe,' said the old gentleman.

There was a smile upon the youth's face as he advanced. Indistinct visions of rook pie floated through his imagination. He laughed as he retired with the bird – it was a plump one.

'Now, Mr Winkle,' said the host, reloading his own gun. 'Fire away.'

Mr Winkle advanced, and levelled his gun. Mr Pickwick and his friends cowered involuntarily to escape damage from the heavy fall of rooks, which they felt quite certain would be occasioned by the devastating barrel of their friend. There was a solemn pause – a shout – a flapping of wings – a faint click.

'Hollo!' said the old gentleman.

'Won't it go?' inquired Mr Pickwick.

'Missed fire,' said Mr Winkle, who was very pale – probably from disappointment.

'Odd,' said the old gentleman, taking the gun. 'Never knew one of them miss fire before. Why, I don't see anything of the cap.'

'Bless my soul!' said Mr Winkle, 'I declare I forgot the cap!'

The slight omission was rectified. Mr Pickwick crouched again. Mr Winkle stepped forward with an air of determination and resolution; and Mr Tupman looked out from behind a tree. The boy shouted; four birds flew out. Mr Winkle fired. There was a scream as of an individual – not a rook – in corporal anguish. Mr Tupman had saved the lives of innumerable unoffending birds by receiving a portion of the charge in his left arm.

To describe the confusion that ensued would be impossible.

To tell how Mr Pickwick in the first transports of emotion called Mr Winkle 'Wretch!' how Mr Tupman lay prostrate on the ground; and how Mr Winkle knelt horror stricken beside him; how Mr Tupman called distractedly upon some feminine Christian name, and then opened first one eye, and then the other, and then fell back and shut them both – all this would be as difficult to describe in detail, as it would be to depict the gradual recovering of the unfortunate individual, the binding up of his arm with pocket handkerchiefs, and the conveying him back by slow degrees supported by the arms of his anxious friends.

Abridged from The Pickwick Papers, *by Charles Dickens, 1837*

HOLY GRAIL

THE HOLY GRAIL for gun collectors is a rare over-and-under wildfowling 12-bore called the Zenith that was manufactured during the 1950s by London gunmakers Robert Churchill.

The Zenith was a heavy duty monster with a curious side opening lever. Churchill's was persuaded to produce the gun by a Turkish millionaire client called Abbas Celal, who spent much of his time shooting duck and geese in Turkey. His guns took an enormous battering thanks to the ridiculously heavy loads he put in them. He had so far managed to destroy a Boss, a Holland and Holland and a Westley Richards.

Eventually Celal came to Churchill's in despair and they produced the Zenith. Only two were made. One is in a private collection in America but the original Turkish gun has disappeared. Do you know where it is?

EXALTED BY DESOLATION

'The shooter to whom loneliness is abhorrent will never make a fowler. Indeed, one might go further and say that he to whom loneliness is not refreshing, who does not feel exalted and uplifted by contact with desolation, had better stick to the company of his kind upon moor and stubble.'

From the 1921 book Sport In Wildest Britain, *by Major Hesketh Vernon Hesketh-Prichard (1876-1922)*

✳ Hesketh-Prichard was considered the best rifle shot of his generation. A year into the First World War he was given the unusual job of 'sniping expert' to the British Army. Britain's sniper looked like amateurs when compared to the Germans. Hesketh-Prichard set up a sniper school in Normandy and used his considerable pre-war sporting experience to put his men through a rigorous programme of everything from rifle maintenance to fieldcraft and camouflage. He insisted that his instructors spend time in the trenches themselves so they knew what they were talking about.

Hesketh-Prichard treated sniping like deer-stalking. He called it 'hun hunting' and he issued his men with the best civilian rifles and 'scopes often funded from his own pocket. He was awarded the MC and DSO.

PROTECTION

An indication of the classlessness of shooting in America is the fact that every single state has passed hunter protection legislation protecting sportsmen from the interference of animal rights extremists. The law states that anyone who knowingly or intentionally interferes with the legal taking of a game animal by another person is committing an offence.

Challenges by protesters have so far failed in the courts. And in a 2005 landmark case an Indiana couple, Frederick and Rosanne Shuger, were convicted of interfering in a deer hunt. They had yelled obscenities, slammed car doors, and blown their car horn in order to scare away the quarry.

America's pro-gun lobby the National Rifle Association can be thanked for campaigning for the legislation. 'Our hunting heritage is under attack by uninformed, misguided people who wish to impose their values on society,' they say.

ST. PARTRIDGE

'Well, this is friendship! What on earth brings you here, old fellow? Why aren't you in the stubble celebrating St Partridge?'

From the novel Robert Elsmere, *by Mrs Humphry Ward, 1888*

✳ Back in Victorian times 1 September, the opening of the partridge season, used to be known as St. Partridge Day. The quote above implies that the season began after the harvest was in and guns could cross the fields without damaging crops.

COMMON AS KINGS

KING EDWARD VIII was the last person you wanted on a shooting party. He was odiously self-centred and suffered from such grandiosity that he actually appeared rather bad mannered and common.

Most people only invited Eddie to shoot on grounds of snob value, in the hope that they would receive a return invitation to Sandringham. A fine example of his abominable rudeness concerned a late season grouse shoot at the Earl of Home's place at The Hirsel in Berwickshire.

The King was shooting on Leadhills, one of the most consistent and prolific moors in Scotland. It was a snowy day and His Majesty was suffering from a sniffle.

The then Lord Home's grandson, the late Sir Alec Douglas-Home, (British Prime Minister 1963 to 1964) recalled in his autobiography, 'It was one of those rare occasions when everything had gone according to plan, and large numbers of grouse had been collected in an area from which they were bound to return through the line of guns.'

The beaters began to walk towards the guns…whereupon the King announced that he was cold and wanted to go home. Immediately!

Protocol demanded that everyone had to go with him. But this was before the days of walkie-talkies and there was no way of stopping the beaters who continued their march. As guns were returned to their cases and the long-suffering guests left the butts, wave upon wave of grouse streamed over the silent line. Sir Alec reported, 'My father said that it was the only occasion on which his loyalty and that of his friends was severely strained.'

GUNDOG RULES

TOP BRITISH POINTER-RETRIEVER TRAINER GUY WALLACE
GIVES HIS THREE GOLDEN RULES FOR TRAINING A GUN-DOG:

1. Life to a dog is either black or white. There are no shades of grey. If it does well you praise it and if it does wrong you rollock it.
2. A dog is being trained consistently twenty-four hours a day. There is no point in giving it half an hour's square bashing every evening and then letting it do whatever it likes for the other twenty-three-and-a-half hours. Similarly it is either always allowed up on the furniture or never allowed on the furniture or it is always allowed to 'break its drop' (get up unbidden from the SIT) or never allowed to break its drop.
3. Let it train itself but (paradoxically) never let it get away with anything.

Wallace adds that to train a dog you must act dumb. 'Dogs are not intelligent (thank God!) And do not have human powers of reasoning. They merely associate one experience with another and build these experiences up as they go along and they also think completely in the present tense. The oft-quoted example of the dog running off and getting a hiding when he returns (usually accompanied by the explanation that "He knows 'e done wrong", which is a load of cobblers) makes the point to a "T".'

From The Versatile Gundog, *by Guy Wallace, Sportsman's Press, 1995*

DON'T BE A CLOWN

'Any gundog puppy should be accustomed to an unloaded gun being carried during training sessions long before the lesson is taught and should be brought up from before its ears are open to accept loud noises such as metal feed bowls being banged on the concrete, hands clapped etc… Introduction to gunfire should not be taught until the pup is at least nine months old and therefore old enough to cope with it… . It is worth going to some trouble to get this lesson right as the trainer only has one chance. The clown who fires a 12-bore over the pup's head at seven weeks old to see if he is gunshy deserves all he gets but that mentality usually ruins any pup anyway. Always assume that all gundog pups are potentially gunshy.'

From The Versatile Gundog, *by Guy Wallace, Sportsman's Press, 1995*

THE CLAY PIGEON

THE CLAY PIGEON was invented by an American called George Ligowsky at Cincinnati, Ohio, in 1862. He got the idea after watching children skimming sea shells off the beach at Coney Island. Ligowsky recognised that the inverted saucer shape gave the shell its stability in flight. A perfectly circular saucer would provide even greater stability.

Much to Mr Ligowsky's irritation his first clays 'rang like a bell' when shot, but he soon perfected his device which he promoted using expert shooters in Buffalo Bill's Travelling Wild West Shows.

Ligowsky's disc flew flatter and faster than previous inanimate targets such as its predecessor the glass ball. The first clays were heavy things that took a lot of breaking. An Englishman named McCaskey soon made them easier to smash by substituting Ligowsky's ground clay and water for river silt and pitch. Limestone later replaced the silt and today's clays are still made of limestone and pitch.

Ligowsky's invention filled every need. It could be made to different sizes and degrees of hardness. It was compact and easy to transport. It sailed smoothly in flight and, unlike the glass ball, the broken shards eventually dissolved into the ground.

Shooting clubs in Britain and America installed traps to throw the clays. Rules were drawn up and contests staged. England's first big clay pigeon shooting competition was the Great Anglo American Match held at Hendon Gun Club in 1901. Prize money totalled £1,000, equivalent to £74,000 today.

Skeet shooting, originally known as 'shooting round the clock', began in the grounds of a kennels in Andover, Massachusetts, in 1920. A shooting magazine offered a prize of $100 for the most appropriate name for the new sport. Ten thousand entries poured in. The winner was a Mrs Gertrude Hurlbutt of Dayton, Montana, who suggested 'skeet,' an old Scandinavian word meaning 'shoot.'

﹡ Ligowsky's early clays faced stiff competition from a flying target named the Peoria Blackbird produced by a shooting man called Fred Kimble.

Kimble, born 1846, began shooting as a child in Illinois where he became known as the state's best duck shot. He spent his early twenties experimenting with boring out gun barrels and he is credited with inventing the first choke-bore shotgun. (Although this is disputed in Britain where a Newcastle-upon-Tyne gun maker called William Rochester Pape filed a patent for a choke bore two years earlier than Kimble's invention.)

Kimble didn't like Ligowsky's clay targets because they often failed to break. Kimble developed a saucer-shaped target made from a combination of coal tar and pitch. He toured the country taking part in shooting exhibitions to promote his product and two million were sold in two years.

However, the name backfired when animal rights lobbyists thought that the inventors were using live blackbirds. A supply of the targets were sent to Boston for a big shoot. The local newspaper ranted, 'Thousands of Peoria blackbirds have been wantonly slain by a lot of heartless men calling themselves sportsmen, and nothing has been done about it. Must a bird become a pigeon to get protection? Hasn't a Peoria blackbird the same right to live and enjoy life as a pigeon? Isn't it just as cruel and heartless to cripple a poor little blackbird? We want the Humane Society to investigate this outrage and bring the perpetrators to account.' When the editor realised his howler, he printed a grovelling apology

The Blackbird's success dwindled when rival firms began producing similar targets more cheaply. Kimble tried to sue other manufacturers for stealing his idea. He lost thousands of dollars on lawyers. He gave up making the targets and continued to invent. But he was beset by bad luck. He made a mallard duck call... which was patented by a man he loaned it to. Thousands were sold. A dental electric vibrator was copied by four manufacturers before Kimble could patent it, and the design of the throwing arm of a clay target trap he developed was still in use thirty years later. None of these earned him a bean.

Kimble continued to shoot superbly into old age. Aged ninety-one he broke ninety-eight out of one hundred clays at the Union Pacific Gun Club in Los Angeles. He died in 1941 aged ninety-five.

DON'T GET TOO EXCITED

'Do not be surprised if you do not shoot up to your usual form when you are tired or not in quite perfect health. A very small thing will upset your shooting. If you are of an excitable temperament, you must combat this as much as possible, for when excited you will not shoot well. Never take a shot in a hurry, as you are likely to do if excited, for the chances are that you will miss.'

From Shooting on A Small Income, Charles Walker, *Archibald Constable, 1900*

THE PURPOSE OF LIVING

'One of the most difficult improvements ever undertaken is that of trying to persuade the English clergy that they receive their salaries for the purpose of living in their parishes, and preaching to their people, instead of shooting partridges in Norfolk, or playing whist at Bath.'

From the London Magazine, *1825, by an anonymous writer called 'C'*

BRITISH GAME SEASONS

GALLINACEOUS BIRDS

Red Grouse	12 August to 10 December
	Northern Ireland: 12 August to 30 November
Ptarmigan	12 August to 10 December
Black Grouse	20 August to 10 December
Capercaillie	1 October to 31 January
Pheasant	1 October to 1 February
	Northern Ireland: 1 October to 31 January
	(cocks only; hens can only be shot under
	Department of Environment licence)
Red-legged (French) Partridge	1 September to 1 February
	Northern Ireland: May only be shot under Department
	of Environment licence.)
Grey (English)Partridge	1 September to 1 February
	Northern Ireland: Protected

WADERS

Snipe	12 August to 31 January
	Northern Ireland: 1 September to 31 January
Jack Snipe	Northern Ireland: 1 September to 31 January
	Elsewhere in Britain: Protected
Woodcock	1 October to 31 January
	Scotland: 1 September to 31 January
Golden Plover	1 September to 31 January
Curlew	Northern Ireland: 1 September to 31 January
	Elsewhere in Britain: Protected

GEESE

Greylag	1 September to 31 January (extension in Great Britain to 20 February in areas below the high water mark of a spring tide)
Pink-footed Goose	Same as greylag
Canada Goose	Same as greylag
White-fronted Goose	Scotland and Northern Ireland: Protected England and Wales: same as greylag

DUCK

Mallard
1 September to 31 January (extension in Great Britain to 20 February in areas below the high water mark of a spring tide)

Wigeon — Same as mallard
Shoveler — Same as mallard
Pintail — Same as mallard
Gadwall — Same as mallard
Teal — Same as mallard
Goldeneye — Same as mallard
Pochard — Same as mallard
Tufted — Same as mallard
Scaup — Northern Ireland: 1 September to 31 January
Elsewhere: Protected

PIGEONS

Woodpigeon — No close season
Collared Dove — Great Britain: no close season
Northern Ireland: Protected
Feral pigeon — No close season

CORVIDS

Magpie, Crow, Jay, Rook, Jackdaw — No close season

ASSORTED PEST BIRDS

Coot and Moorhen — Great Britain: 1 September to 31 January
Northern Ireland: Protected
Gulls — No close season
Starling and House Sparrow — No close season

❋ It is illegal to shoot game during the period from one hour after sunset to one hour before sunrise.

LOW FREQUENCY PHEASANTS

PHEASANTS have such good hearing at lower frequencies that during the Blitz birds would start crowing in Hampshire while London was being bombed. Likewise, in Japan, pheasant crowing can warn of an earthquake.

However, pheasants are unlikely to become members of Mensa. They are far less intelligent than ducks, geese or pigeons. Hence they can be driven over a line of Guns and still return to the same wood later that day. What makes them such good game birds is their natural wariness combined with good eyesight.

A MOMENT OF TERROR

Shooting writer Giles Catchpole offers this imaginary conversation between a novice guest gun and the head keeper.

'Marvellous day, Mr King, thank you very much indeed.'

'Very happy you enjoyed it, sir. I thought the birds did well.'

'Indeed they did. Well up and nicely spread out. A deal too good for me anyway.'

'Well, sir, I gather you had a few. You had a nice walk, anyway.'

Catchpole explains: 'Loosely translated this means, "It was reported to me that you were safe enough to walk and shoot at the same time and that you made it the length of the wood with only a single woodcockian moment of terror for my staff, and shot well enough following emergency tuition."'

From Birds, Boots and Barrels, *by Giles Catchpole, Swan Hill Press*

WHEN NOT TO SHOOT A DOG

Shoot lunch gossip in 1808 centred on a prominent court case between a shooting man called Mr Vere and a Welsh landowner called Lord Cawdon.

Mr Vere was travelling past Cawdon's estate when his luggage got loose. He was forced to halt his carriage. But as his servants were securing the loose cases his gundogs managed to break free. The setters shot off onto Cawdon's land in pursuit of a hare.

Minutes later shots rang out and Vere found his dogs shot dead by Cawdon's gamekeeper. Having failed to extract any compensation from Cawdon, Vere took his case to the High Court. The judge Lord Ellenborough ruled that the shooting of the dogs was unjustifiable and illegal. After all, no hare had actually been killed. He advised a 'liberal compensation.'

The jury granted Mr Vere the extraordinarily high damages of £100 – nearly £6,000 in today's money. A year later Lord Cawdon appealed...and lost again. Judge Ellenborough commented, 'Is it to be endured that a man's dog, or any other animal, shall be shot because he merely follows a hare?'

STARTLING

THE RECORD BAG FOR STARLINGS is around 500 killed in one shot by our old friend the legendary Lt. Col. Peter Hawker. He achieved this amazing feat at 5 am on 26 October 1825 on a lake at Alresford, Hampshire, with his 'great double gun loaded with 30 ounces of shot.' Two hundred and forty three starlings fell dead immediately and between two and three hundred were found the next day dead in the reeds.

✳ Hawker advised that men who shot as much as he did should wear gloves to prevent their hands from becoming calloused. This was for reasons of good taste only. 'Many people fancy they cannot shoot in gloves, and consequently their hands become as coarse as those of a gamekeeper, which, utterly as I abhor dandyism, I must yet observe, is not quite in unison with the appearance of a perfect gentleman.'

CLIPPED SPARROWS

NOT FOR BUNNY-HUGGERS: in his best-selling 1860 shooting manual *The Dead Shot*, the author, who calls himself 'Marksman', recommends that shooting sparrows from a pigeon-trap is good practice for partridge shooting.

'If a very small portion of the tips of the feathers in each wing be clipped off with a pair of scissors, or if a portion of their tails be cut off in the same manner, it will make them fly so steadily, and so much like young partridges, that it will be as good practice as he can make before the shooting season commences.'

Another method to make a sparrow fly in a direct line is to cut a hole in a piece of paper about four inches square and slip it over its head. 'The paper forms a collar which impedes their flight considerably.'

FLYING DOGS

Early nineteenth century dog breeders believed that the best time for gundogs to couple was when the moon was in Aquarius or Gemini. The 1816 sporting manual *The Shooter's Guide* explains: 'The whelps so begotten will never become mad, and the litter will have more dog than bitch whelps.'

Meanwhile, if you wanted to encourage your dogs to copulate, you should give both dog and bitch the following: 'Two boiled heads of garlic, half a castor's stone, and almost a dozen Spanish flies, in a pipkin that holds a pint of water.' Add mutton to taste. The author of this recipe declared, 'If this be given to the bitch three or four times, it will not fail to make her proud; and if given to the dog will incline him to copulate.' Hardly surprising after a dozen Spanish flies.

THE DEVIL

At the 1870 gundog trials at Vaynor Park, Bangor, Wales, a competitor called Mr Thomas Ellis entered a retriever called The Devil into the elderly dog class. The Devil, a fine beast with vast whiskers like an otter hound, won easily. His victory reached the ears of Welsh Church elders who publicly denounced Mr Ellis for glorifying Satan. Mr Ellis made sure he did not get into trouble again. The next year he entered a dog…called Country Rector.

THE EYNSHAM POACHING SONG

Three Eynsham chaps went out one day
To Lord Abingdon's Manor they made their way
They took their dogs to catch some game
And soon to Wytham Woods they came
Laddie-i-o, Laddie-i-o Fal-de-ral over a laddie-i-o
We had not long been beating there
Before our spaniel put up a hare;
Up she jumped and away she ran,
At the very same time a pheasant sprang.
We had not beat the woods all through
When Barrett, the keeper, came in view;
And when we saw the old beggar look
We made our Cassington Brook.
When we got there 'twas full to the brim,
And you'd have laughed to see us swim,
Ten feet of water, if not more;
When we got out our dogs came o'er
Over hedges, ditches, gates and rails,
Our dogs follows us after behind our heels;
And you can all say what you will
We'll have our hares and pheasants still.

Traditional folk song from the upper Thames

STUFFING

Eighteenth century shooting depended greatly on the quality of the wadding you stuffed down your barrel. The firmer the wad, the greater the explosion. The English tended to use tissue paper or wool. But the French, ever closer to the land, discovered that lichen worked best. The French sporting writer Gervais-Francois Magne de Marolles recommended in 1781 that you should use 'a very fine moss of a greenish grey colour found adhering to apple trees.'

AK NOT OK

Mr Jim Zumbo, 67, an American TV personality and longtime contributor to shooting magazine *Outdoor Life*, was sacked in 2006 after writing an article in which he described the AK47 rifle as a 'terrorist weapon.' His comments were prompted by the fact that across America thousands of gun fanatics use AK47s, AR-15s and other assorted assault weapons to shoot nothing more dangerous than deer and prairie dogs.

Mr Zumbo, a barrel-chested macho man who lives in a log cabin, wrote: 'Maybe I'm a traditionalist, but these things have no place in hunting. I'll go so far as to call them terrorist rifles. I've always been comfortable with the statement that hunters don't use assault rifles. We've always been proud of our "sporting" firearms. Game departments should ban them from the prairies and woods.'

But you simply don't get away with that sort of reasonable view in America. Mr Zumbo lost his cable TV show and was forced to write a grovelling retraction after the country's rednecks accused him of being a commie bastard, or words to that effect.

'Horse's ass', 'ass pimple', 'this Zumbo guy is toast' and the curious 'Zumbo ain't nothing but an anti bambi-zapper' were some of the more printable comments that appeared on pro-gun blog spots around the United States.

Paradoxically, the extraordinary outpouring of rage provoked by Zumbo's mild observations led anti-gun campaigners to point out such angry (and quite obviously certifiable) people shouldn't be allowed anywhere near semi-automatic assault weapons in the first place.

✳ Author's note: No gentlemen would dream of going stalking with an AK47. What's wrong with a Rigby?

A THOUGHT…

'The fascination of shooting as a sport depends almost wholly on whether you are at the right or wrong end of the gun.'

P.G. Wodehouse

T.C.S.

'Shooting is extremely difficult if one attempts to satisfy the most severe critic of all, namely the man who shoots.'

'The primary factor in the choice of a gun is the length of the purchaser's pocket.'

'It is clearly better to aim greatly too much in front than a little too much behind.'

'Snipe shooting is the fly fishing of the shot gun. Very few men ever excel in snipe shooting. The actual aiming at a snipe is the difficulty. He may be there when you aim, but is not there when the shot arrives.'

'No bird gives a more easy shot than a woodcock...and at the same time none is so often missed.'

'Trap shooting...can scarcely be described as attractive, except to pot and spoon hunters, but to non competitors two hours of it must be woefully boring.'

All words of wisdom from George Teasdale-Buckell, doyen of Edwardian shooting, and author of the 1907 handbook *The Complete Shot*. George T-B was a tremendous egotist known by some as That Complete Shit.

BLAZING BAMBI

AN ENTERTAINING SHOOTING HOAX began circulating on the internet in early 2002. The story, which originated on the Associated Press wire service, said that in an effort to protect deer, the anti-blood sports group People for the Ethical Treatment of Animals (PETA) had dressed up more than four hundred deer in orange da-glo vests in the Ohio forest.

The idea was that hunters – who by law have to wear orange vests – would not dare shoot in case they shot one of their own. The story went on to say that a sporting goods store had tried to thwart PETA by paying a bounty for every vest taken from a dead deer. It all turned out to be complete nonsense and it only served to enrage PETA. Because, as wags pointed out, a deer dressed in orange makes a marvellous target.

THE COST OF SHOOTING

THE MAHARAJA DULEEP SINGH was one of the greatest pioneers of British driven game shooting.

Having come to the throne of the Punjab aged five Duleep was deposed by the British six years later. He spent his early teens under house arrest in Lucknow. Such was the fear that Duleep would eventually return to the Punjab and start a rebellion, his British captors proceeded to Anglicise him. He was allowed no contact with Indians and he was bombarded with stories about how wonderful England was.

The British efforts paid off. Duleep arrived in Britain in 1854 aged sixteen. And by his twenties he was on the way to becoming a proper country gent, acquiring sporting estates in Suffolk and Perthshire. He was the first Indian prince to arrive in Scotland – he ran a record-breaking grouse moor at Grandtully in Perthshire – and he endeared himself to the locals by wearing highland costume and becoming rather good at reels. He earned the nickname 'The Black Prince of Perthshire.'

Duleep received a substantial pension from the British government in compensation for his lost fortune. The British also bought him the seventeen thousand-acre Elveden estate on the Suffolk/Norfolk border near Thetford. And for the next twenty years he proceeded to spend his pension turning Elveden into one of the finest shoots in England. He employed armies of gamekeepers to rear vast numbers of pheasants. The finest shots in England, from Walsingham and Ripon to Leicester and the Prince of Wales, became his friends.

Queen Victoria gave Duleep the rank of a European prince. She adored Duleep. It is said that she once scolded him for refusing to wear woollen underwear during cold weather. She feared that his tropical background would cause him to die of hyperthermia. Duleep told Her Majesty that he could not wear wool next to his skin because it made him itchy. 'It makes me long to scratch,' he explained, 'And you would not like to see me scratching myself in your presence.' Victoria dropped the subject.

Alas, even a pension of the size given to Duleep does not go far if you are as obsessed by shooting and social climbing as he was. And by 1880 the money was running out.

Duleep asked the Government for more. But they declined. Nor would they return the famous Koh I Noor diamond which had been confiscated from his family. Rather than face the shame of not being able to entertain his smart shooting friends in the manner to which they had been accustomed, Duleep set out for India where he planned to gather an army to restore his family lands.

The British stopped him at Aden and he was turned back. After a brief stay in Russia, where he tried unsuccessfully to persuade the Czar to invade India and install him as ruler, he settled in Paris where he lived until his death in 1893 aged only fifty-five.

Sons Prince Freddy and Prince Victor brought his body back to Suffolk. Duleep was buried in Elveden churchyard close to his beloved coverts. The estate was sold to pay his debts. However, the Maharajah's memory lives in Thetford where a statue of him was unveiled by Prince Charles in 1999 in recognition of the money that he ploughed into the area during his lifetime.

Whatever Duleep's shortcomings, he has gone down in history as one of the quickest shots Britain has ever seen. Nobody could fire so rapidly as he did. Indeed, while lecturing his sons on the intricacies of shooting, he uttered the immortal line: 'Cartridges are meant to be let off.'

❋ Duleep's record was 780 partridges to his own gun at Elveden on one day in September, 1876.

HOW TO DEAL WITH A GUN SHY DOG

'If a dog shows any nervousness on the report (of a gun), let him walk with an attendant a hundred paces distant, and every time you squib off the gun proceed to call him and pick up a bird, which can be laid down when he is not looking. He will probably overcome his fear in his anxiety to take part in a performance so interesting to him, and can gradually be brought nearer and nearer to the shooter...

'But the really bad case, such as the dog that goes off as hard as he can, tail between legs till he reaches his kennel, must be considered hopeless. We never saw or heard of a complete cure...except a mutton chop served with strychnine sauce.'

Tough words from nineteenth century shooting expert Sir Ralph Payne-Gallwey

❋ Sir Ralph had advice on how to stop your young dog from mauling retrieved birds. 'Have ready prepared a piece of hedgehog skin, and secure it firmly by elastic straps or twine to a recently killed partridge. Give the dog to an attendant, and substitute the bird just dropped for the other. Now let the retriever seek and find, and from pricking his mouth he will soon learn to pick up game tenderly, whether alive or dead.'

TRYING TOO HARD

LORD DE GREY, LATER MARQUESS OF RIPON, was one of the finest shots in Victorian England. But he was also a perfectionist with a strong desire to be top dog in the shooting field.

Late one evening, while staying for a shooting party at Lord Desborough's Hertfordshire estate Panshanger, de Grey was in the library with two long-suffering loaders practising changing over from gun to gun. He thought everybody had gone to bed, so he was horrified when a female houseguest, Lady Edith Balfour, walked in looking for a book.

'He was not pleased at being discovered,' Lady Edith recalled, adding archly, 'In those days it was considered more praiseworthy to excel by unforced aptitude.'

OWL MUCH BETTER WITH ONIONS

There are few historical accounts of owl shooting. But one instance, in 1794, concerns Raisley Calvert, a louche young man in his early twenties who happened to be the best friend of the poet William Wordsworth.

Having shot his owl Calvert brought it back to his house in the Lake District where Wordsworth, and fellow Lake poet Robert Southey, later Poet Laureate, were staying.

Calvert and Wordsworth wanted to put the owl in the bin. But Southey thought there would be no harm in cooking the bird on the basis that the damage had already been done.

Southey recalled, 'As there was no sin in eating the owl, I ordered it to be dressed and brought in, in the place of game that day at dinner. It was served up without the head, and a squat-looking fellow it was, about the size of a large wild pigeon but broader in proportion to its length.'

It was a filthy dinner. Southey added that 'the meat was more like bad mutton than anything else' and Wordsworth 'was not valiant enough to taste it.'

Southey's conclusion? 'If you ever have an owl dressed for dinner, you had better have it boiled, and smothered with onions, for it is not good roasted.'

Calvert played an important part in Wordsworth's career. On his death from tuberculosis in 1795 Calvert left Wordsworth £900 with a note that he hoped his friend would devote himself to poetry. The money enabled Wordsworth to embark on a career that would have been otherwise impossible.

HOW TO DEAL WITH ANTIS

THIS ADVICE COMES DIRECT FROM THE BRITISH ASSOCIATION OF CONSERVATION AND SHOOTING. PLEASE MEMORISE!

Shooting, properly carried out, is a lawful activity.

On private land it is a criminal offence (aggravated trespass) to obstruct or disrupt anyone pursuing a lawful activity. It is also an offence to intimidate someone so as to deter them from taking part in that activity. Blocking an access road, walking in front of the guns, threatening or attacking the guns can all be criminal offences.

The police have the power, in most circumstances, to arrest anyone committing a criminal offence.

Trespass itself (being on land without permission) is a civil offence. The police have no power to act. A landowner or his agent may ask trespassers to leave, and subsequently may use 'reasonable force' to remove them. 'Reasonable force' can be interpreted in many ways by the courts, and the use of force could leave you open to prosecution. The police are only likely to intervene in removing trespassers to prevent a breach of the peace. Trespassers are not required to give their name and address to anyone. The police may only demand these details when a criminal offence has been committed.

A court injunction can be obtained against repeat offenders. Someone who contravenes an injunction can be held in contempt of court.

In Scotland, legislation relating to trespass is more complicated, and it is sometimes argued that the offence does not exist. However, anyone causing actual damage or disruption may be requested to leave. There is also recourse to an interdict, similar to an injunction, to guard against repeat offences.

A public right of way (such as a footpath) exists only to allow the passage from A to B. It does not give the right to demonstrate or indulge in any other activity. This has been upheld in court.

Criminal damage falls into two types. It is a criminal offence to destroy or damage property belonging to another without authority or permission. (Simple criminal damage.) It becomes aggravated criminal damage if there is an intention or a possibility that the damage could endanger life. These offences could apply to damage to snares, traps, release pens or any other shoot equipment.

A common assault can be defined as a threat or offer to commit violence against an individual. More serious offences, such as actual bodily harm up to attempted murder, are committed when injuries are sustained.

Intent. The police have power to intervene if they believe a criminal offence is about to be committed.

BASC insist you should plan ahead and be prepared for trouble. 'It is essential that all shoots have a prepared plan for dealing with saboteurs or demonstrators. Everyone taking part in the day must understand what to do in the event of disruption. One person, the shoot captain or keeper, must take charge, make adequate preparations and take the key decisions if an incident occurs. In vulnerable areas, where saboteurs are known to be active, plans should be discussed with the police in advance.'

Before the Shoot…

• In vulnerable areas, make contact with the local police. If appropriate, provide them with a list of shoot dates, a contact name and telephone number and indicate where shooting may take place.

• Avoid placing pegs and markers in advance in areas which may draw undue attention. Consider placing guns personally or setting out pegs for each drive. Decoy pegs might be placed in areas where shooting will NOT take place.

On the shoot day ensure there will be…

• At least two mobile phones, programmed with the most effective police contact number. The police will advise. 999 should be used if necessary.

• A camera, notebook and pen for recording evidence. A disposable camera will be sufficient. Descriptions of individuals are particularly important. It may be necessary to identify an offender in court, when they are more smartly dressed, and link them to particular actions. Record details of any vehicles used. (NB Antis hate being photographed since many are likely to be on a Special Branch database as known animal rights terrorists.)

• Establish a set procedure for halting a drive. Make sure all the guns, beaters, pickers-up and others are briefed. All firearms must be immediately unloaded, placed in slips and kept secure on the person. They must never become involved in a dispute, nor fall into the hands of an unauthorised person.

• Guns should congregate at a convenient spot, avoid confrontation and carefully record any provocative or illegal acts, no matter how minor. The demonstrators will be seeking to provoke reaction and retaliation. A calm, measured response is essential.

• Ensure that all vehicles are left secure, with no firearms or ammunition at risk. Consider security for properties and equipment which may be isolated during the shoot, such as the keeper's house, rearing and release pens etc.

• Take care of dogs. Put them on leads as soon as an incident seems likely to occur. Be aware that noxious sprays and chemicals have been used against foxhounds. Provocation may even extend to trying to aggravate the dog.

FINALLY, REMEMBER IT'S YOUR WORD AGAINST THEIRS!

The shooter has a lot to lose if taken to court. The saboteur often has nothing to lose. Many make a career out of protest and actively seek to be arrested. Often, if reliant on state benefits, they can end up paying little in the way of fines or fees. Through experience they know how to exploit the legal system and will seek to cause the shoot members to cause an offence.

Be aware that they may be filming you, and may spit, swear and use any form of provocation in order to provoke a violent response. If this happens, they have won.

When making notes, difficult as it may be in the heat of the moment, look for details which will identify a hooligan when the balaclava is replaced by a smart suit in court. Record details of the actions of individuals rather than groups, and make notes of the effects of those actions on those around you. Record a date and times where possible. This information will be invaluable in court.

UNSUNG HERO

GREATEST UNSUNG SHOOTING HERO of the Victorian/Edwardian era is a little-known fellow called Mr Reginald Rimington-Wilson.

Old Etonian Rimington-Wilson, cavalry officer, landowner and all round good egg, managed to find his way into second on the list of the twelve best game shots in Britain that appeared in *Bailey's Magazine of Sports and Pastimes* of 1903.

To have even appeared in the '03 *Bailey's* list was in military terms similar to winning the Victoria Cross. To have come second after only Lord Ripon was a remarkable achievement for a commoner. It was the highest accolade that any keen shot could ask for and throughout the country houses of England there were gasps that someone born without a title had reached such an exalted position.

Rimington-Wilson was famous for shooting a record bag of 2,843 grouse for nine Guns during six drives in one day in August 1913 on his moor at Broomhead in Yorkshire. The day was recorded as 'fine, with an east wind.' TheGuns included the Earls of Powis, Darnley and Westmorland and m'Lords Savile and Lewisham.

Though only 4,000 acres, Broomhead, on the outskirts of Sheffield, was a showpiece shoot. It produced stupendous bags. Rimington-Wilson, who shot with Boss single-trigger guns, stressed that his big bags were not made for their own sake, but simply because the grouse were on the moor and it was the only way to get them. To hunt for grouse in small numbers would have meant driving most of them away never to be shot.

That Rimington-Wilson, 1852 to 1927, was a very great shot there is no doubt. He was even famous enough to be caricatured by Spy in *Vanity Fair*. And like his rival Lord Ripon he was a first class billiards player. It is worth noting how often expert billiards and shooting go hand in hand.

Broomhead is still owned by the Rimington-Wilson family.

⁂ Rimington-Wilson was once asked for his shooting tips:

1. When shooting at fast, crossing birds, look at the place you are going to shoot, not at the bird.

2. For near grouse bring up the gun in the nearest way, without swing, and shoot right at the bird. But for far off birds you must swing.

3. For pheasants, get behind them, race your gun to the front of the bird without stopping the gun to inquire whether you have passed the body of the bird because such a pause will mean you shooting behind. However, in a deep gully when you have no time to swing it is quite acceptable to snap shoot. And if the first shot doesn't hit, then the second probably will.

4. Do not use choke bores – distance they increase the range is paid for by lack of killing power.

✳ Rimington-Wilson's staff were also handy with a gun. In 1923 a Broomhead underkeeper called Dyson killed a blackcock and a stoat with one shot. It was remarkable shooting. The stoat had attacked and seized the bird which was flying away. Dyson killed them both.

✳ Another Rimington-Wilson fact. One of his early seventeenth century ancestors at Broomhead is credited with shooting the first grouse on the wing.

PERISH THE THOUGHT

'Only fast women shoot'
Queen Victoria.

BOEING OVER

Britain's most unorthodox shooting syndicate took place during the 1950s alongside the runways at Heathrow Airport. A nearby market garden provided good root cover and the guns consisted mainly of airport officials and a team of doctors from Slough.

Lord Thomas, former chairman of BOAC, recalled, 'As many as twenty guns would turn up, assembling in the intermittent flash-light of the ghastly green neon beacon which marked the whereabouts of London airport to air traffic.'

The drives consisted of pushing coveys of partridge over the high wire perimeter fence. Bags averaged around fifty head, including wild pheasants and a few snipe from the western end of the runways. The birds took little notice of the aircraft, but it was unnerving for the guns. Thomas explained, 'It could be a strange feeling to draw a bead on a rising cock pheasant and then to find a trans-Atlantic aircraft in line with one's barrels.'

EXCEPTIONALLY ROBUST

This gruesome article appeared in the *Spalding Free Press* in 1898: 'A remarkable accident is under treatment at Spalding Johnson Hospital. A farm servant named Arthur Doades, aged fifteen, was in a field with a gun scaring birds, and when reloading the weapon and ramming down the charge, the gun exploded and the ramrod passed through the boy's head. It entered his forehead, and came out at the top of the head, carrying his cap with it, alighting some distance away. He was found in an unconscious state, and at first no hopes were entertained of his recovery; but though the injury to the brain is serious, he has now recovered consciousness, and there is a slight chance that he may get better. The case is regarded at the hospital as a most remarkable one and the fact of his still being alive is attributed to his exceptionally robust constitution.'

Arthur's 'robust constitution' evidently saved him. For after spending fifteen weeks in hospital he was discharged and lived for the next twenty-eight years.

TAKE A DEEP BREATH...

If you weren't fortunate enough to inherit a fine English sidelock shotgun, here are the prices for a new one. Expect to dig deep into the piggy bank if you require more bling in the form of extra engraving. Prices inclusive of VAT:

Fabbri – North Italian gun maker Fabbri of Brescia make only a few guns each year at around £100,000 each. Perhaps a little too glitzy for your English sporting gent.

Holland and Holland – £55,424 basic cost for a Royal side-by-side 12, 16 and 20-bores. A 28 or .410 will cost you nearly £3,000 more. Plenty of optional extras ranging from around £4,000 for a single trigger mechanism to £400 for a leather butt pad. A Royal 12-bore with all the trimmings will come to £66,000.

James Purdey and Sons – At £54,637 for a classic side-by-side 12, 16 or 20 a Purdey is slightly cheaper than a Holland. But a .410 is a whacking £61,100. A top whack gun can cost £80,000.

Boss and Co. – £70,000 will buy you a beautiful Boss 12, 16 or 20-bore with almost every option you can think of except for specialist engraving. Just as posh as a Holland or Purdey.

William Evans – Keenly priced at £41,000 for a best grade London side-by-side sidelock 12-bore with the firm's distinctive bold scroll action. A discreetly smart gun. If an English gentleman these days was in a position to buy a new pair of guns he is likely to be tempted by William Evans on the basis that their pieces are almost as good as Purdey or Holland but arguably better value.

E.J. Churchill – A perfectly acceptable London shotgun ranging from £40,000 to £60,000 for a top of the range Premiere model.

Watson Brothers – Around £43,000 for a top of the range classic gun with your own choice of engraving. A relatively obscure City of London gun maker that has been going since the late nineteenth century and is known for its coffin-shaped, rounded action guns.

Westley Richards – £31,137 for a 12, 16 or 20-bore. A single trigger 12 with best walnut stock is a reasonable £36,000. But you must remember that this is a Birmingham gun with none of the cache of the London boys. A fine, workmanlike fowling piece nevertheless.

A.A Brown and Sons – £32,000 upwards for a special order side-by-side 12-bore from this Birmingham company that has been going since 1938. Most shooting folk haven't heard of Browns but that doesn't stop the company charging around £50,000 for their most expensive weapons.

McKay Brown – A reasonable £35,000 for a basic round-action 12-bore from Scotland's finest gun maker. Expect to pay up to £15,000 extra for specialist engraving.

PARTRIDGE FACT

Far from being indigenous to Britain, the so-called 'English' grey
partridge actually originated in Hungary – and indeed in
Europe greys are often referred to as 'huns'.

NOT BUILT THAT WAY

THE MIDDLE-CLASS BOOM IN SHOOTING towards the end of the
nineteenth century caused some interesting social problems. Men were now
in the habit of 'taking a gun' on a Yorkshire moor for perhaps a month at a
time. Often a chap answered a newspaper advertisement, arriving at the
shooting box without knowing any of his fellow guns.

The Victorian shooting writer Augustus
Grimble advised caution when entering into
such arrangements. 'Anyone taking a gun on
a moor should make sure his future host is a
gentleman and a good sportsman,' he
stressed, adding that you should stipulate
that it should be men only. 'If each Gun
brings his wife, and several ladies hitherto
strangers to each other get boxed up on a
Scotch moor, ten miles from shops or
neighbours, there are almost certain to be
"ructions"; and small wonder either, for a
duller life for ladies can hardly be imagined
– botany, entomology, and mild trout
fishing are the only outdoor amusements
open to them.'

Grimble was open minded enough to
concede that ladies could relieve the boredom by learning to shoot. But he
added that 'few are built that way and the writer is convinced those who do
shoot rarely find any real pleasure in the matter, and as soon as they have
shown us poor men they can do it if they choose, and wipe our eyes as often
as they please, most are content to rest on their laurels.'

From Shooting and Salmon Fishing and Highland Sport, *by Augustus Grimble*

THE PASSENGER PIGEON

The greatest single pigeon stand was by a Dr A. Welford of Ontario, Canada, who one day in 1870 killed four hundred passenger pigeons from dawn until 10am. Dr Welford recalled that the air was black with flock upon flock of pigeons heading eastwards. Millions of birds filled the air. They shadowed the sun like clouds and the roar of their wings resembled low rumbling thunder. Having run out of powder for his flintlock, the doctor proceeded to knock down a number of low-flying pigeons with a stick.

What is remarkable about this event is that forty-four years later the passenger pigeon, once the most numerous bird on the planet, was extinct. This was due to massive over-shooting and reduced food supplies as a result of forests being cut down as people settled across the United States. The last passenger pigeon, a female, died on 1 September 1914 in Cincinnati Zoo.

AN ACRE OF HARES

THE LARGEST NUMBER OF HARES EVER RECORDED in one place was by the social commentator William Cobbett. He noted in his acclaimed *Rural Rides* that on 22 October 1822 he saw 'an acre of hares' in a field near the village of Netherhaven, Wiltshire. 'Mr Beach (the landowner) received us very politely. He took us into a wheat stubble close by his paddock; his son took a gallop round, cracking his whip at the same time; the hares…started all over the field, ran into a flock like sheep, and we all agreed that the flock did cover an acre of ground.'

NEVER EVER

The entirely unremarkable seventh Duke of Roxburghe, who did little throughout his life other than shoot, was once peppered in the face by the equally unremarkable seventh Earl of Chesterfield, who likewise did little in his life other than shoot. Roxburghe was hit so hard that the blood ran down over his shirt. What was remarkable about this incident is that the pair were 180 yards apart.

Which proves that you should never *ever* point your gun at anyone.

SWALLOWS

One of the most bizarre shooting achievements on record is twenty swallows shot with a flintlock pistol by Captain Horatio Ross. This feat took place in the mid-nineteenth century at Ross's family seat Rossie Castle, near Montrose, and was the result of a £100 wager Ross struck with a friend that he could not shoot twenty swallows in one day.

Such was the number of swallow nests in the towers of Rossie that the match was finished before breakfast.

Ross was named after his father's great friend Horatio Nelson. Rossie, a Regency Gothic pile built circa 1800, was of such immense construction that it took two attempts to blow it up when it was demolished in 1952.

ROYAL ENDORSEMENT

'Properly managed shooting has never put any game species at risk of extinction, moreover, it has made a significant contribution to the conservation of the countryside and to the economy of rural areas – and continues to do so.'

Quote by HRH The Duke of Edinburgh

TECHNICAL POINT

A shotgun needs to weigh about 6 lb for every ounce of shot that it is likely to fire.

SPORTING BIRDS

ON 31 JANUARY 1914 a member of the Royal Dublin Golf Club managed to kill a flying Brent goose with a golf ball. It was at the sixth hole and the player was using a mashie. In May 1909 a lady at Hendon Golf Club killed a swift in a similar manner. In September 1920 golfer Mr Hugh Watt brought down a seagull at Gullane, Scotland and the following year Mr S. Olssen whacked a kestrel about sixty feet from the ground with a golf ball at Kettering links. Over in America Mr Tom McHugh killed a low-flying pelican with his ball while golfing in 1924 at Lincoln Park, San Francisco, and in Rangoon, Burma, 1929, Mr Norman Patterson scored a golfing right and left when he managed to kill two birds, identified as meadow pipits, with one ball. Tennis and cricket balls have also been known to claim feathered victims.

✳ On 6 January 1923, a hare being pursued across Aldershot golf course by the Aldershot Command Beagles was hit and knocked over by a ball driven by Mr Ernest Stroud. The Master of Beagles was rather cross.

POETRY

EVEN BACK IN VICTORIAN TIMES shooting legend Lord Ripon predicted that game shooting might not survive. 'Maybe a generation will spring up to whom all these things will be a closed book,' he wrote in a moment of pessimism. 'But when that day comes, England will lose her most attractive and distinguished feature and one of her most cherished traditions. For the England of whom the poets have sung for many centuries will have ceased to exist.'

THE RUDE GUN

The author David Hudson, in his book *The Small Shoot*, tells the story of an obnoxious gun he once met. He was the type that is unfortunately found in so many syndicates these days.

The first drive of the day was a duck pond to which this syndicate member took great exception. He had paid to shoot pheasants and therefore he expected six pheasant drives and not five pheasant drives and one duck drive. He made a hell of a fuss... and then proceeded to shoot more ducks than anybody else.

Hudson remarks, 'Afterwards and in private it was made clear to the gun that whatever he might feel about the organisation of the shoot it was not done to start a row in public, and most particularly not in front of our host, just at the time when the guns were required to go as quietly as possible to take up their places around the duck pond.'

So how should syndicates deal with bounders like this? Hudson reports that a quiet word with the shoot captain or a discussion at the Annual General Meeting, if the syndicate has such a thing, usually does the trick. He adds, 'Most guns, finding that the way a shoot is run is not to their liking, would simply vote with their feet and not renew their membership at the end of the season. Open rebellion against the management simply raises the possibility that they will not be invited to join again even if they should want to do so.'

From The Small Shoot, *by David Hudson, Swan Hill Press, 2003*

THEN AND NOW

Then:
Up goes a guinea, bang goes a penny, down comes half a crown.

Now:
Up goes twenty-five pounds (plus VAT), bang goes fifteen pence, down comes twenty-five pence...if you're lucky.

THE LINCOLNSHIRE POACHER

When I was bound apprentice in famous Lincolnshire
Full well I served my master for more than seven years
Till I took up to poaching, as you shall quickly hear
Oh, 'tis my delight on a shiny night in the season of the year.

As me and my companions were setting of a snare
'Twas then we spied the gamekeeper, for him we did not care
Far we can wrestle and fight, my boys and jump out anywhere
Oh, 'tis my delight on a shiny night in the season of the year.

As me and my companions were setting four or five
And taking on 'em up again, we caught a hare alive
We took a hare alive my boys, and through the woods did steer
Oh, 'tis my delight on a shiny night in the season of the year.

I threw him on my shoulder and then we trudged home.
We took him to a neighbour's house, and sold him for a crown
We sold him for a crown, my boys, but I did not tell you where
Oh, 'tis my delight on a shiny night in the season of the year.

Success to ev'ry gentleman that lives in Lincolnshire
Success to every poacher that wants to sell a hare
Bad luck to ev'ry gamekeeper that will not sell his deer
Oh, 'tis my delight on a shiny night in the season of the year.

Traditional English folk song

SEXIST STUFF

'A lady begins to know she is shooting well when the men
stop telling her that she is.'

From A Shooting Man's Creed, *by Sir Joseph Nickerson*

ANNIE OAKLEY

FINEST LADY SHOT OF THE VICTORIAN ERA was Annie Oakley, later immortalised by Irving Berlin in the musical *Annie Get Your Gun*.

Born Phoebe Moses in a log cabin on the Ohio frontier in 1860, Annie began shooting game aged nine to support her widowed mother and siblings. By the age of twelve she could shoot the head off a running quail.

Word spread and aged sixteen Annie entered a Cincinnati shooting match with celebrity marksman and vaudeville performer Frank E. Butler. Annie won by one point. She also won Frank's heart and they married a few years later. Frank recognised that Annie was far more talented and gave up the limelight to become her manager.

In 1885 Annie and Frank joined Buffalo Bill Cody's Wild West Show. Annie, at only five feet tall, rapidly became the star attraction. She could shoot a dime tossed ninety feet into the air, and in one day she shot with a .22 rifle 4,472 out of 5,000 airborne glass balls.

The Wild West Show toured Europe. Wilhelm, Crown Prince of Germany, invited Annie to shoot a cigarette from his lips. Annie easily accomplished this although she remarked later that had she shot the Prince and not his cigarette she might have prevented the First World War.

Even into middle-age Annie was still shooting like a dream, breaking ninety-eight clays out of one hundred on her fiftieth birthday with her cherished Ithaca trap gun. So what was the secret of Annie's shooting? She told the *New York Sun* in 1892: 'The ability to trigger the shot at just the right time is a feeling,' adding sagely, 'But practice and experience helps…'

✳ One of the first gunmakers to have its own shooting school offering simulated game shooting with clay targets was Charles Lancaster of London. While Annie Oakley was touring England with the Wild West Show in 1887 she popped into Lancaster's shooting ground to have a lesson. Quite what Lancaster had to offer Ms Oakley is uncertain. But Lancaster's 1889 book *The Art of Shooting* includes an illustration of Annie receiving instruction from him.

HONESTY

'When I take a gun in hand the safest place for a pheasant is just opposite the muzzle.'

Sydney Smith (1771 to 1845), English essayist and clergyman

A RECIPE FOR ROOK PIE

Ingredients:
six rooks;
pepper and salt;
three hard boiled eggs;
½ lb of rough puff pastry;
1 pint warm water;
1 oz butter;
1 lb steak;
½ oz of instant powdered gelatine;
1 oz flour.

Wash rooks well, taking care to remove the livers and backbones. Cut into neat joints and the steak into pieces. Toss in flour, pepper and salt. Fry the rooks in hot butter and put onto plate, brown the steak, add warm water and simmer 1 hour. Put the rooks into the mixture and simmer for 1 hour longer. Boil eggs, remove shells and cut into quarters. Put the rooks, meat and eggs into a pie dish, pour gravy over gelatine and stir till dissolved. Pour over rooks and when cold, cover with pastry, decorate, brush with a beaten egg and bake for ½ an hour. Pour in the gravy and serve cold.

Important note: Rooks are covered in fleas. Before you skin a rook put animal fat around your wrists. When the fleas hop off the rook onto you they will stick in the fat and go no further.

❧ Countryman's Rook Note 1: ❧

'A crow in a crowd is a rook.
A rook on its own is a crow.

❧ Countryman's Rook Note 2: ❧

Traditionally, rooks can sense the approach of death.
If a rookery is abandoned, it is said to bring bad
luck to the family that owns the land.

IMPOSSIBLE TO KILL

An unnamed Edwardian wit, having been a shooting guest at Powis Castle in Wales where the pheasants were known for their stratospheric qualities, noted: 'Pheasants did not fulfil the condition of their existence, which is to end –and before they are old and tough – on the dinner table. The birds, often invisibly impossible to kill, ran greater risk of dying of lead poisoning from eating the shot on the ground than from any external application of the same.'

FOR SHOT DOGS

IN THE EARLY NINETEENTH CENTURY setters and pointers were quite often accidentally shot by their masters while putting up partridges and grouse. The 1816 book *The Shooter's Companion*, by B. Thomas, recommends the following remedy for a shot dog: 'Oil of turpentine, oil of chamomile, and aqua vitae, of each two ounces, mixed well together with half a pint of linseed oil.' This compound to be rubbed well into the wounds.

FLESH AND FEATHERS

Lord Walsingham warned that on big shooting days guns and spectators should keep an eye out for falling pheasants. He recalled an incident from about 1880 at Riddlesworth, Norfolk: 'A Waterloo veteran was heard to exclaim, in tones of supreme resignation, "I am shot! I am shot!" when nearly three pounds of flesh and feathers descended on the side of his head from a considerable height, stopped by the unerring gun of a certain noble duke.'

LUNCH CART

'The best lunch cart we ever saw was invented by our friend Sir Edward Lawson, of Hall Barn (near Beaconsfied, Bucks). It started in life as an Irish car, only to be developed into something much better: it has a place for eatables, an ice well, and two seats and benches, which take to pieces and pack into the car. When in use the usual seats are the buffets, the boards on either side, on which the feet should rest are tables, at which the benches enable the shooters to sit and eat in great comfort.'

From Shooting and Salmon Fishing and Highland Sport,
by August Grimble, 1902

NOT DONE, OLD BOY

One day in September, a sabbath morn,
I shot a hen pheasant in standing corn.
Without a licence – 'twere hard to plan
Such a cluster of crimes against God and man!

*By the poet Richard Monckton Milnes (1809 to 1885),
later first Baron Houghton*

DEFECTIVE TASTE

One of the most popular rural elegies of the eighteenth century was the 1767 poem *Partridge Shooting* by Francis Fawkes. Fawkes was best known for his translations of Greek classics such as the *Argonautica* and *Sappho*. Here is a verse from *Partridge Shooting:*

> Enough! Enough! No longer we pursue
> The scattered covey in the tainted dew.
> No more we charge, nor new excursions make,
> Nor beat the copse, the bean field, nor the brake.
> O pleasing sport! Far better prized than wealth!
> Thou spring of spirits, and thou source of health,
> Thou giv'st, when thus our leisure we employ,
> To life the relish, and the zest to joy.
> O may I still on rural pleasure bent
> Rove devious in sequestr'd fields of Kent;
> Ease, study, exercise successive blend,
> Nor want the blessing of a cheerful friend!

While the ruddy-face yeomen of the sequestr'd fields of Kent might have enjoyed this cheesy ditty, the critics were less kind. 'There is, in our opinion, a want of judgement in everything this author writes,' spluttered an anonymous contributor to the *Monthly Review*. 'Nothing can be a stronger argument of the false taste than to join the ridiculous with the pathetic.'

Sighting such lines as 'There we retrieve and spring them one by one, Sweet transport to the lovers of the gun', the reviewer concluded, 'Those passages we have pointed out are sufficient to prove the defective taste which disqualifies the author for original composition. We would advise him henceforward to confine his powers to translation because, by following another, he will not be liable so frequently to err.'

A WORK OF ART

Someone once defined the English side-by-side shotgun as 'a work of art which feels lighter than it really is.'

THE FIRST HEATHER BURNER

The man credited with introducing heather burning in order to increase grouse numbers is Donald Ross, head keeper to the fifth Duke of Portland. In 1859 Ross decided to experiment setting fire to the moorland at Welbeck in the Nottinghamshire Peak District. This had a remarkable effect on the grouse who fed hungrily off the regenerated heather shoots. By 1871 the annual bag at Welbeck had climbed from the mere hundreds to 2,230 brace.

Meanwhile, Portland was so reclusive that he seldom went outside in the daytime (except on shoot days) and preferred to live in a warren of subterranean rooms that he built specially beneath Welbeck Abbey.

Keeper Ross got little thanks from his boss. After a lifetime's sport on a massive scale – the partridge bags at Welbeck were particularly enormous – Portland wrote in the final pages of his gamebook: 'When I look back…I am quite ashamed of the enormous number of birds that we sometimes killed. This is a form of shooting which I have no desire to repeat.'

THE ONLY TIME

The ONLY time when you are permitted to point your gun at anybody is when your shooting instructor asks you to raise your gun and point it at the bridge of his nose in order to see which of your eyes is dominant.

THE ROYAL CONSCIENCE

After a pig-out of a day's shooting at Lord Burnham's Buckinghamshire estate Hall Barn, when the bag totalled 3,937 pheasants, King George V turned to his son the Prince of Wales, later Edward VIII, and remarked, 'Perhaps we overdid it today.'

THE OVER-AND-UNDER

The method of putting one barrel above the other – over-and-under – actually came before the invention of the side-by-side.

The first over-and-under barrels appeared on early seventeenth century German wheel-lock pistols. These were cumbersome affairs. After firing the first barrel you had to turn the gun upside down in order to fire the second barrel. The introduction of the flint lock made things much easier and the next range of German pistols featured rotating barrels. After the top barrel had been fired the lower barrel was rotated and discharged by the same lock mechanism.

By the 1700s this 'turn over' system was popular on both pistols and muskets. Side-by-sides only began appearing in France from the mid-1700s.

The first modern over-and-under shotguns were produced by London gunmakers Thomas Boss in 1909 and James Woodward in 1911. Then Frederick Beesley produced his Shotover model, the most perfectly designed over-and-under ever produced. But these English guns never took off, and the over-and-under as we know it today was invented by an American, John Moses Browning. Sadly Browning never lived to see his invention in general use as he died in 1926, the same year that the gun went into production.

THE TRUE COST OF SHOOTING

SHOOTING WRITER GILES CATCHPOLE tells the entertaining story of a chap who left his shoot syndicate's annual bill lying on the breakfast table while he went to recover from the shock.

Unfortunately, his wife saw it and went ballistic when she realised how much he was spending on shooting. 'The worst part is that the letter was only asking for a twenty-five per cent deposit,' Catchpole says. 'If she had found out the true extent of the damage, I dare say there would have been murder done. Shooting is an expensive business. Like marriage. Or divorce.'

From Birds, Boots and Barrels, *by Giles Catchpole, Swan Hill Press, 2002*

COLLECTIVE NOUNS

A tok of capercaillies
A covert, raft or codgery of cootes
A flight of cormorants
A murder or hover of crows
A head of curlews
A flight, dole, dule, pitying or prettying of doves
A flush, team, dopping (when diving), plump, paddling (on water), flush (brood), badelynge, or brace of duck
A gaggle, flock, nide, skein or wedge (when flying in a V) of geese, (but a gang of brent)
A covey, brood (single family) or pack (large group) of grouse
A band or party of jays
A tittering or tiding of magpies
A sord, flush (on land), sute or puddling (on water) of mallard
A covey or bew of partridges
A nye, or ni or nid (large group), bouquet (when flushed) or brace (pair) of pheasants
A brood or pack of grouse
A flight or flock of pigeons
A congregation, leash or wing of plovers
A bevy or covey of quail
A parliament, building or clamour of rooks
A walk (at rest) or wisp (in flight) of snipe
A host, quarrel or tribe of sparrows
A murmuration of starlings
A spring, coil, knob or raft of teal
A dread of terns
A company, bunch, coil or knob of widgeon
A trip of wildfowl
A fall, covey, flight or plump of woodcock (woodcock are always a couple, never a brace)
A sege of herons, and of bitterns
A whiteness of swans
A herd of swans, cranes and curlews
A muster of peacocks
A watch of nightingales
A charm of goldfinches

ADVANCE THE MUZZLE AND YOU
STRIKE HER DEAD

IN 1727 GEORGE MARKLAND, a fellow of St John's College, Oxford, wrote a much-acclaimed poem called *Pteryplegia – The Art of Shooting Flying*. It contains what are possibly some of the first pieces of advice on how to shoot well…with a flintlock at least.

⁂

WHEN A BIRD comes *directly to your Face*, Contain your Fire a while and let her pass, Unless some Trees behind you change the Case. If so, a little Space above her Head Advance the Muzzle, and you strike her dead. Ever let Shot pursue where there is room; Marks hard before thus easy will become.
　　BUT WHEN the Bird *flies from you in a Line*, With little Care I may pronounce her thine: Observe the Rule before, and neatly raise Your Piece til there's no *Open under-space* Betwixt the Object and the *Silver Sight*; Then send away, and timely stop the Flight.

TH' UNLUCKY *Cross Mark*, or the *Traverse Shoot*, By some thought easy (yet admits Dispute, As the most common Practice is to Fire Before the Bird) will nicest Time require: For, too *much* Space allow'd, the Shot will fly All innocent and pass too nimbly by; Too *little* Space, the Partridge, swift as Wind, Will dart athwart and bilk her Death behind. This makes the Point so difficult to guess, 'Cause you must be exact in Time or miss. In other Marks there's a less desp'rate Stake, Where the swift Shot will surely *Overtake*…

FULL FORTY Yards or more to th' Left or Right The Partridge now *Obliquely* takes her Flight. You've there th' Advantage of a *Sideling Line*; Be careful, nor her inward Side decline: Else just behind the Bird the Shot will glance: Nor have you any Hopes from *Flying Chance*. Last is the Mark which is styled *Circular* There's nothing more required but steady Care T'attend the Motion of the Bird and gain The best and farthest *Lineal Point* you can; Carrying your Piece around, have Patience till The Mark's at best Extent, then fire and kill…

⁂

Markland then issues a warning about drinking too much at lunchtime...

BUT HOLD, my Spirits fail! a Dram, a Dram, A Sup of Vigour to pursue the Game! Enough, enough. A Gulp too much is worse Than none at all, like one help'd over his Horse. Sportsmen, beware! for the superfluous Glass Will blunt the Sight and ev'ry Object glaze, Whilst all Things seem around one undistinguish'd Mass. Th' unpointed Eye once dull'd, farewell the Game: A Morning Sot may shoot, but never aim. Marksmen and Rope-dancers with equal Care Th' insidious fasting Bottle shou'd forbear. Else each who does the Glass unwisely take E'er Noon a false and fatal Step will make; The first will *Turkeys* slay, and make *Pigs squeak*, The latter, ten to one, will break his Neck.

PHEASANT'S REVENGE

On 11 November 1921 a pheasant managed to stop the 10.37am Great Western express train from Welshpool to Shrewsbury. The bird struck the locomotive and dislodged a pipe operating the vacuum brake thus putting the brake into operation. The train ground to a halt throwing passengers to the floor.

FALSE TALE

'The picturesque story of the sportsman who killed 1,999 snipe to his own gun in a season in the Orkney Islands and then shot himself in the misapprehension that he was the two thousandth snipe is not true. The bag is incorrect (he killed more than the coveted number) and, although the sportsman died by his own hand, it is understood that he had weightier troubles than snipe to worry him out of existence.'

From Record Bags and Shooting Records, *by Hugh S. Gladstone, 1922*

※ Gladstone tells another good story of a shoot in Scotland. At the end of a drive one of the guns asked the keeper if he could do a role call of the beaters. The keeper did so and reported that all were present and correct. 'Very good,' the gun said. 'In that case I have shot a roe...'

TEETOTAL

Victorian Scottish sporting writer John Colquhoun explains how best to tackle an arduous day of walked up grouse:

'There are a few rules which a man not accustomed to climb hills will find his account in observing, if he would escape the suppressed smile of derision which his flagging will be sure to excite from the sturdy hill-man who carries his bag.

One is to eat a very light breakfast; another, to drink as little as possible; but especially no spirits and water. If you can hold out without drinking 'til your luncheon your thirst will never be very oppressive; but once begin, and the difficulty of passing a clear brook is tenfold increased.

The provision basket should only consist of a cold fowl, or a few sandwiches, and a bottle of table beer or light ale. When you again begin your exertions make your attendant carry a bottle of strong tea, without cream or sugar, which will more effectually quench your thirst than a whole flask full of spirits and water to correspond.

Should any object to this "teetotal" system, a little fruit may be no bad substitute.'

Colquhoun adds that when he first started shooting he thought the spirit flask almost as indispensable as the powder flask. But experience proved that this was a bad idea. 'Nothing more expends the remaining strength of the half worn out sportsman than a few pulls at the liquor flask. He gains a temporary stimulus, which soon ends in complete exhaustion.'

✳ The nineteenth century American sporting writer Elisha Lewis had similar things to say about the consumption of alcohol while shooting: 'A flask of good spirits is an important accompaniment, but should be resorted to as seldom as possible. The use of liquor during active exercise often creates an unnatural thirst, which, if indulged in to an extent sufficient to produce a flush on the cheek or a glow on the body, will most assuredly make the eye uncertain or the hand unsteady, and, moreover, prove otherwise injurious by opening the pores of the system and making the shooter more susceptible to the effects of cold. The truth is that no drink insures better health, and produces a more equable tone throughout the whole system, than the exclusive use of unadulterated water…'

LEGAL GROUSE TRIVIA

VICTORIAN SCOTTISH LANDOWNER and serious grouse shot Sir Donald Campbell won an Edinburgh court case towards the end of the nineteenth century forcing the Post Office to hang boards from the newly-erected telegraph wires that went across his moor. This was a result of grouse killing themselves by flying into the wires. The 18 x 6 inch wooden boards warned the birds of danger ahead so that they could take evasive action.

BUNNY BONANZA

The world's biggest rabbit round-up was on 13 March 1892 when around 30,000 jack rabbits were killed at Fresno, California. Eight thousand beaters drove the animals into a large staked coral where they were knocked on the head.

BORN NOT MADE

'I am quite convinced that the real wildfowler is born not made. By this I do not mean that you must necessarily have been brought up to the sport from very early days, but that you need have the love of the wild, free places of the earth deeply ingrained in your nature, and be one of those who count the game above the prize…There are not many game shots who would consider, say, three brace of pheasants or partridges a noble return for much labour and discomfort, yet to many a shore fowler the same number of mallard or wigeon would count as the sort of red-letter day which only comes once in a number of years. Yes, without a doubt, the fowler must be born, but to those who have the magic in their blood the call of the saltings and mudflats is infinitely stronger than that of the stubbles and rootfields, or even the lure of the heather-clad moors.'

From Letters To Young Sportsmen, *by Major Kenneth Dawson, 1920*

AN ANTI WRITES

'I think I've found the place I want to move to. It's only a couple of miles away – a farm with two hundred odd acres of arable land and some woods where posh people could come and shoot that most stupid of all birds, the pheasant. Except that if I bought the place I'd arm the pheasants too and maybe lay down some of those trip mines that were so effective in Angola. Extreme Pheasant Shooting, I could call it, and display bits of unfortunate rich people in glass cases in the hallway.'

Rod Liddle, Times *columnist, October 2003*

ANOTHER ANTI WRITES…

ADOLF HITLER had much in common with the 'antis' of today. In a polemic from September 1942 he explained his dilemma with regards to banning blood sports: 'Personally, I cannot see what possible pleasure can be derived from shooting…I have never fired at a hare in my life. I am neither poacher nor sportsman…(But) if I excluded poachers from the Party, we should lose the support of entire districts.' On another occasion Hitler remarked sourly: 'I am no admirer of the poacher… particularly as I am a vegetarian.'

GETTING PRIORITIES RIGHT

IN THE YEARS BEFORE WORLD WAR TWO Air Marshal Hugh Dowding was given the job of building a chain of radar receivers. Many of these were to be positioned on moorland across the north of England and Scotland.

However, Dowding's task was not made easy thanks to the numbers of shooting men in positions of power. A 1936 British government 'siting specification' for radar stations stated that sites must be 'secure against sea bombardment, inconspicuous from the air and it is furthermore essential that they should not gravely interfere with grouse shooting…'

EARLY AIR GUN

The eighteenth century sporting writer William Daniel recalled a nasty incident with an early air gun that was being used to shoot rabbits at a park in Essex. A servant was pumping air into the weapon with such force that a screw snapped and the copper shot burst sideways out of the barrel. Luckily it missed the owner of the gun, a Mr Tyssen, and crashed into some nearby trees. Mr Tyssen vowed never to pick up the thing again. The gun was consigned to the rubbish tip.

SIR WILLIAM CONGREVE

As you pull your Purdey's trigger and that pheasant crashes down, the name of Sir William Congreve may mean little to you. But his is one of most important names in the development of the shotgun.

Sir William, artillerist and inventor of the first war rockets, held the title of Comptroller of the Royal Laboratory at Woolwich towards the end of the Napoleonic Wars. In 1815 he was awarded a patent for the standardisation of gunpowder. Powder quality could now be controlled to give a more calculable efficiency. This was to become extremely important with the introduction of the cartridge.

Sir William loved anything that went off with a bang. Indeed, he was in charge of the lavish London firework displays following the victory at Waterloo.

CELEBRITIES WHO SHOOT...

On second thoughts, no, we won't name them and give yet more ammo to the antis...
Suffice to say that famous people enjoy shooting just as much as we common folk.

KNOW YOUR PUNTER

Let days can be a minefield. Here are some pithy words of caution from shooting writer David Hudson:

If a team of guns has contracted for a 150-bird day it is not advisable to see them with 140 pheasants in the game cart at the end of the first drive. Nor is there any point in sending a succession of fifty-yard high screamers over a team of relatively novice guns who are liable to end the day demoralised, disappointed and well short of their agreed bag limit. Certainly, if the keeper has been using a clicker to count the shots, and can point out that they fired nine hundred cartridges for the hundred pheasants hanging in the game larder, then it can be argued that the shoot has fulfilled its side of the bargain by providing the guns with the opportunity to shoot the full, agreed bag. But it would have  been better all round if drives had been chosen that offered slightly easier pheasants so that the guns could end the day satisfied with their results.

From Gamekeeping, *by David Hudson, Swan Hill Press, 2006*

LYING BITCH

Arch-fibber Baron Jerome Munchausen (1720 to 1797) whose absurdly exaggerated exploits were described in Rudolph Raspe's 1786 book *The Adventures of Baron Munchausen*, is said to have ridden astride a cannon ball, travelled to the moon and pulled himself out of a swamp using his own hair.

Munchausen also fancied himself as an expert shot. Apart from boasting that he killed 126 duck with one barrel, he claimed that his bitch Diana was the best-trained pointer in the world. Munchausen said he once found her motionless in the same place where he had left her fifteen days earlier pointing a covey of partridges. Unsurprisingly, when the partridges were put up the baron killed twenty-five in a single shot.

THE CZAR'S GUN

THE HIGHEST PRICE PAID for a secondhand gun was in 2007 when a weapon called The Czar's Parker fetched nearly £150,000 at auction in America.

Guns manufactured by Connecticut gunmakers Parker Brothers during the first half of the twentieth century are coveted collector's items that routinely sell for tens of thousands of dollars. There is nothing outstandingly different about the Czar's gun although it was surrounded in mystery and some collectors doubted whether it even existed.

The 12-bore was made for Nicholas II, Russia's last czar, in 1914. The gun was ordered by an officer in the Imperial army and it is not certain whether it was meant as a gift or at the request of the Czar, or indeed whether Nicholas even knew about it. But the dimensions of the gun were clearly designed to fit a man of Nicholas's short stature.

The gun was on its way to Russia, reaching the docks of New York harbour, when Germany declared war on Russia. The onset of the First World War sent the gun back to Parker Brothers factory in Meriden and the firm lost contact with the Russian officer in question. Several months later, having given up on the Russian deal, Parker Brothers sold the shotgun to a New York banker, Henry Sanford. The vendor was a member of the Sanford family.

Had the Czar actually touched this much-hyped weapon it would have put another £50,000 on the price. The firearm was bought by Minnesota gun dealer Jack Puglisi who said he had no plans to sell on the gun, but would 'fondle it and play with it and shoot it as well'.

APOCRYPHAL STORY

AN AMERICAN WAS ON AN ENGLISH SHOOT when he was spotted aiming at a cock pheasant running along the ground.

'Surely you are not going to shoot it?' gasped the picker-up.

'No way,' said the American. 'I'm gonna wait 'till he stands still.'

THE KEEN SHOT'S MISCELLANY

CADS TAKE NOTE!

'A person who rears no pheasants himself, and puts down food to allure those reared by his neighbour, is guilty of a very unsportsmanlike and dishonest act. Unfortunately, as the law stands, there is no redress so long as the wrong doer abstains from "trespassing in pursuit", there being no property in game until reduced into possession by the occupier of the land on

which it is shot by him or his friends. The only plan is to have the bounds beaten so as to keep the birds from straying as much as possible, and to see that there are no thick hedgerows on the boundary which would be likely to harbour them.'

From The Second Field Book Of Country Queries, *Pelham Books, 1989*

FULL MOON FEVER

THE OCTOBER FULL MOON is traditionally known as the 'woodcock moon' for this is the time when the birds migrate. Long after they should have settled down for the night, the brightness of the full moon encourages male woodcock to keep calling their mates and doing display flights.

The reality is that woodcock do not usually appear in large numbers in Britain until November. They migrate from Scandinavia, Russia, and the Baltic States. Cold weather drives them to Britain and Ireland

in search of a milder climate and soft ground – they feed on earthworms and insects sucked out of the earth by their long bills, hence the nickname 'bog-sucker.'

The woodcock's two needs are good nighttime cover and worms – the birds can consume up to a third of their body weight each night in worms. Some woodcock consider Britain too cold and head further south. They can be found in North Africa and parts of the middle east, and have been known to visit India and Sri Lanka.

SWEET MUSIC

All the sports of the field are delightful, I own,
But none can with shooting compare;
'Tis a joy that entices the king from his throne,
'Tis a joy that the wisest may share.
The voice of the hound on the breeze of the morn,
The note of the bugle, may please;
The song of the wild bird is sweet from the thorn,
But the gun has more music than these.

Anon, Nineteenth century

OLD STORY

A FRENCHMAN WAS ON HIS FIRST GROUSE
SHOOT on a Scottish moor which happened to be
heavily populated with sheep.

After the first drive the man's host enquired how many
grouse he had shot.

The Frenchman replied, Grouse? Oh non, they are far
too fast. But I have killed five moutons sauvages…'

CHURCHILLIAN ADVICE

A pheasant shot by mistake in September is known as a 'queen partridge.'
At least that was according to legendary 1920s gun maker and shooting
instructor Robert Churchill.

'Don't bury it,' Churchill advised in his book *Game Shooting*. 'Just apologise
as handsomely as you can to your host.'

A PERFECT VOLLEY

An eloquent defence of large scale pheasant shooting appeared in a vast 1890 book called *Birds of Norfolk* by an ornithologist called Henry Stevenson:

The majority of those writers who...can find no milder epithets than 'bloodthirsty' and 'unsportsmanlike' to mark their abhorrence of pheasant shooting, are either practically unacquainted with the working of the system, or are deficient themselves in that necessary coolness and skill without which even pheasants, big as they are, will escape from a perfect volley of double barrels.

Such individuals seem wholly unable to associate the enjoyment of a heavy day's covert shooting with skill in the use of firearms and physical endurance, quite overlooking the fact that amongst the sportsmen accustomed to congregate towards Christmas time at the country seats of noblemen and wealthy squires for the purpose of joining in these great 'battues' (slaughters) are some of the very best shots in the world. If men such as these – and there are many – can enjoy for a change a big day in some well-stocked coverts (where hunting probably is stopped by the frost), one would scarcely term it an unsportsmanlike diversion...and if anyone is inclined to despise the amusement on the ground that pheasants are easy to kill, let him try his hand late in the season at a few old cocks flushed some two hundred yards from the post of the shooter, so that the bird is in full flight when he passes over. The pace is then tremendous!

ODE TO A DUCK

'Tis said that when a mallard chooses her mate
And death, or accident, destroys her lover,
She mourns her loss, submits to fate,
But during that year, chooses no other.

Rather bad nineteenth century poem, Anon

SNOBBY

Snobbier shooting types put the initials PWAG against certain people in their address books. This stands for 'Person With A Grouse Moor.'

THE RUFFORD PARK POACHERS

A buck or doe believe it so A pheasant or a hare Were set on earth for everyone Quite equally to share

So poacher bold, as I unfold Keep up your gallant heart And think about those poachers bold That night in Rufford Park

They say that forty gallant poachers They were in distress They'd often been attacked when Their number it was less

Among the gorse, to settle scores Those forty gathered stones To make a fight for poor men's rights And break the keepers' bones

The keepers went with flails against The poachers and their cause So no man there again would dare Defy the rich man's laws

Upon the ground with mortal wound Head keeper Roberts lay He never will rise up until The final judgement day

Of all that band who made a stand To set a net or snare The four men brought before the court Were tried for murder there

The Judge he said 'For Robert's death Transported you must be To serve a term of forty years In convict slavery'

So poacher bold, your tale is told. Keep up your gallant heart And think about those poachers bold That night in Rufford Park

Traditional English folk song

PARTRIDGE POEM

And now the golden harvest cracks the barn
Whilst at the door stout flail-men bang the corn:
The leazers now have given their gleaning o'er,
The netters too have plentifully swore,
when the shy birds, raised at the sound of down,
Clapped their loud wings, and mocked the horseman's frown.
In the evening's close, soon after Phoebus fall,
Watchful attend the partridge skreaking call.
The coveys for their roosing place prepare,
The old ones send their summons from afar,
And to their scattered young give signals of their care.

From Pteryplegia, or The Art of Shooting Flying, *by George Markland, 1727*

SNOOTY

Shooting's snootiest quote belongs to an unnamed duke who described a fellow nobleman's newly laid out shoot thus: 'Although the birds are always high, wide and handsome, there is no sense of history and it could never be classed as great.'

A HARD WINTER

SO SEVERE WAS THE WINTER OF 1880-81 that starving grouse in Yorkshire ended up looking for food in farmyards. They became so tame that they happily lived alongside chickens. Up in Scotland the birds desperately searched for berries from rowan trees. It is said that when the ten foot snow drifts eventually cleared hundreds of starved grouse were found lying dead beneath the blackthorn bushes.

CONCERNING DOGS

ONE OF THE MOST PRACTICAL PIECES OF ADVICE given by twentieth century shooting pundit Sir Joseph Nickerson concerns dogs. Sir Joseph stresses that you must ensure your dog has had a crap before you take it shooting. There is nothing worse, he says, than a gun arriving at a shoot and his dog promptly dumping on the host's lawn.

Although he probably didn't know it, Sir Joseph was echoing the thoughts of a Regency gamekeeper called John Mayer who included this excellent nugget of advice in his 1823 book *A Sportsman's Directory*: 'When a keeper is going shooting with gentlemen, let him give the dogs a run to empty themselves, previous to their starting as nothing is more disagreeable than seeing the dogs continually stopping in their beat to evacuate.'

IF CHICKENS FLEW WE'D SHOOT THEM TOO…

The great Victorian naturalist and adventurer Charles Waterton explained in his *Essays On Ornithology* why the pheasant made such a good flying target: 'Notwithstanding the proximity of the pheasant to the nature of the barn-door fowl, still it has that within it which baffles every attempt on our part to render its domestication complete. What I allude to is a most singular innate timidity, which never fails to show itself on the sudden and abrupt appearance of an object. I spent some months in trying to overcome this timorous propensity in the pheasant, but I failed completely in the attempt. Young birds learn to feed out of the hand, but fly at the presence of an intruder, be he dog or man. This timidity is an insurmountable bar to our final triumph over the pheasant.'

SERIOUS SPORTSMEN

The most readable Victorian shooting book was *Shooting Field and Covert*, published in 1885 as part of the Badminton Library sporting series. The book was penned by the formidable team of Lord Walsingham and Sir Ralph Payne-Gallwey Bt.

Sir Ralph listed the qualities of character demanded of the serious sportsman:

'He is equally happy whether he be beating a bit of marsh for the chance at the two or three snipe it may contain, waiting in the twilight for an occasional shot at a duck, or standing outside a well-stocked covert from which the pheasants are being driven over his head in scores.'

'Ignorant people imagine that a shooter who is accustomed to take a part in the killing of five hundred pheasants, grouse or partridges, as the case may be, would refuse an invitation to assist in killing a hundred. This is all nonsense; a shooter...would delight in a "small" day, provided his skill were taxed in shooting...'

'A good specimen of the race....usually excels in all the athletic and other amusements dear to Englishmen, such as cricket, riding, fishing, and billiards. He looks thoroughly workmanlike from top to toe, and you will find that all details of his equipment, be they his guns or the buttons of his leggings,

are as perfect as may be for practical use.'

'He is kind and generous to keepers, though never familiar, is devoted to dogs, and is generally popular.'

'When shooting...he goes at once to his post when it is pointed out to him...With him it is never a case of "There go some birds, I must go to my stand and finish my story another time."'

'He *never*, unless directly questioned, alludes to his own skill, though others do not fail to do so, and rather gives the idea that he does not himself know how well he shoots.'

'His game...is never spoilt and so made unfit for food; it is in fact killed clean at all reasonable distances.'

Sir Ralph had only scorn for 'the bad, unsporting shot.'

'He is for ever explaining why he does not shoot better – an explanation that no one cares one jot about.'

'He is no judge of distance, and will as readily fire at a bird or animal eighty paces off. After a long shot he may be seen shading his eyes with his hands as if he expected the bird to drop, and as a suggestion that the said bird was hard hit and will not go far – anything rather than that it should be thought he made a clean miss.'

'Such a shot is usually a jealous one, as he is anxious to get as much shooting as he can so that his bag may not be so scanty as to cause comment, and he is very fond, when he has fired at another man's bird, of exclaiming, as the better marksman drops it and he clean misses it, "There is plenty of shot in that bird, anyway…" thus implying that the bird was equally peppered by both shooters. He will, indeed, even claim it as his if he gets the chance, or say, "I believe that last bird we both shot at was dead before you fired, was it not?"'

'When placed at his peg he paces about cigarette in his mouth and gun over his shoulder, looking meanwhile in an opposite direction to that from which the game must come, and till several birds have perchance passed by him.'

Sir Ralph argued that there could be a middle way…

'There are plenty of merely bad shots who are excellent fellows in every way, who readily admit they are bad shots, who never pretend to be anything else and never will, but who are, nevertheless, thorough sportsmen as well as pleasant and fair shooters, and who behave just as do they good shots, save only in respect of their want of skill in marksmanship.'

❋ It is generally thought that Lord Walsingham was a born killer on the shooting field, interested only in huge numbers. Not so. In *Shooting Field and Covert* he expresses mild disgust for enormous bags: 'It will be generally admitted that all the elements of true sport are wanting when large numbers of pheasants, crowded together in low covert by surrounding beats, rise in continuous flights over guns placed near enough to render the game unfit for food; for although there are some professors of the art who can be trusted even under such circumstances to strike only the necks and heads of the birds, almost without knocking a single feather from their bodies, to the majority of sportsmen such close proximity, if it does not prevent them altogether from attempting to add to the bag, produces a sense of disgust rather than of pleasure.' Lord W concluded that some guns would 'sigh for the old days of pheasant shooting over spaniels and setters, in preference to what they are accustomed to designate mere slaughter.'

ENGLISH DECADENCE

THEODORE ROOSEVELT, keen rough shooter and early twentieth century President of the United States, was sniffy about shooting in England. He remarked, 'Laying stress upon the mere quantity of game killed, and the publication of the record of slaughter, are sure signs of unhealthy decadence in sportsmanship.'

HOLIDAY BY RAIL

Now, when the sportsman is flitting from market and Mammon,
Now, when the courts, swept and garnished, stand silent and lone,
Now, with her challenging grouse, and her sea-silver salmon,
August, of mountains and memories, comes to her own;
Would you gaze into the crystal, and see the long valleys,
Braes of the North, and the rivers that wander between,
Crags with those coating the tint of the ptarmigan tallies?
Come up to Euston tonight about 7.15.

From Green Days And Blue Days,
by Patrick R. Chalmers, Maunsel and Co., 1910

EPITAPH TO MAN AND DOG

In frost and snow, thro' hail and rain,
He scour'd the woods and trudged the plain;
The steady pointer leads the way,
Stands at the scent, then springs the prey;
The timrous birds from stubble rise,
With pinions stretched divide the skies:
The scattered lead pursues the sight,
And death in thunder stops their flight;
His spaniel of true English kind,
With gratitude inflames his mind;
This servant in his honest way,
In all his actions, copied Tray.

*Epitaph to gamekeeper Robert Mossenden, died
1744, on a tablet outside St Mary's church,
Harefield, Middlesex. Tray was the name
of Mossenden's spaniel.*

BAD LUCK ON THE DEER

KING ERNST AUGUST OF GERMANY achieved an amazing record in 1845 when he managed to shoot four roe deer with one shot. The bullet passed through the head of the intended target before striking the others one by one.

MORAL: LISTEN TO YOUR WIFE

SHOOTING'S CREEPIEST TALE concerns twenty-four-year-old Viscount Andover who was staying at a house party in Norfolk in January 1800.

The night before he was due to go shooting Lord Andover's wife Jane had a dream that her husband's gun exploded and killed him. She related this to her husband the next morning. Andover said he'd never heard such bollocks in his life and nothing was going to stop him having a damned good day with his chums.

All went well during the morning but shortly after lunch one of Andover's dogs started playing up. Andover handed his gun to the man behind him while he stooped to catch the dog. Somehow the gun went off and shot Andover in the back. He was carried back to the house where he greeted his wife with the words, 'Dear your dream has come true' and promptly died.

Lady Andover later remarried Admiral Sir Henry Digby who commanded the third-rate ship of the line HMS *Africa* at the Battle of Trafalgar. The couple had a daughter called Jane, a beautiful but wayward girl who became famous for endless affairs with numerous European dignitaries including King Ludwig I of Bavaria and his son Prince Otto, before moving to Syria and settling down with a Bedouin sheik.

Lord Andover would have been grateful that he never had children.

THE MCNAB

A Mcnab, in which you must shoot a stag, catch a salmon and bag a brace of grouse between dawn and dusk on a single day, was named after the mythical poacher in John Buchan's 1925 novel, *John Mcnab*.

The book tells the story of three successful but jaded London high-flyers – barrister, cabinet minister and banker – who issue a challenge to three Scottish estates that they will poach the stag, salmon and grouse from each of them, signing themselves collectively as John Mcnab.

Back in the real world, recent correspondence in *The Field* magazine included the rules for a Royal McNab, which involves bagging a stag, a salmon, a brace of grouse...and the lodge cook. (Although it doesn't count if the cook is also the spouse of the gun.)

There is also talk of an Imperial Mcnab which is a stag, a salmon, a brace of grouse, the lodge cook and the owner of the lodge. Bearing in mind that the owner of a Scottish shooting lodge is often an elderly, hard-up laird with a dubious approach to hygiene, it is unlikely that this will ever be taken up. It will certainly never be boasted about.

❊ On 10 October 1927 Sir Ian Walker, Bt, as a result of a bet, killed two salmon, two stags and two grouse in the Glenavon Forest, Scotland. The salmon were caught by 9.45 am, the stags by 4.30 pm and the grouse just before dark.

Mr George Davey recorded on one day in 1920 a bag of two stags, fifteen grouse and seventeen salmon. He got the stags by 3.30 pm, shot the grouse on the way home and then achieved the salmon by laying out a net in the loch by his house not long before drinks time.

More disconcertingly, in 1921, a Mr Eric Parker had just landed a 26 lb salmon out of the Boldside Water, near Melrose, Scotland, when he was knocked down by a cock pheasant shot by a member of a nearby shooting party. To make the picture complete, at that very moment across the loch the Buccleuch Hounds broke over the hill in full cry.

A GOOD STAG

PRIZE FOR MOST BIZARRE ENTRY IN A GAME BOOK goes to Lt. Colonel Peter Hawker who on 2 July 1823 noted: 'I made a ridiculously good double shot this evening at a bat and a stag beetle.'

This is probably the first and last time that anyone has boasted about shooting a stag beetle.

GOD'S MERCY

AN OLD COLONIAL SHOOTING TALE concerns the bored English commissioner of a district in rural India who, looking for something to do, attempted to organise a quail shoot. Being an inexperienced shot the official managed to hit not one single quail. When asked by another gun what the man's bag had been, his Indian attendant replied, 'Oh, the Commissioner Sahib shot very well…but God was merciful to the birds.'

BECAUSE THEY LIKE TO HAVE A DOG

In his 1907 book *The Complete Shot*, George Teasdale-Buckell, dryly witty observer of Victorian and Edwardian shooting, offers nine reasons why people buy retrievers such as labradors:

- Because they like to have a dog.

- Because they like to collect more game than they shoot.

- Because they do not like to leave wounded things to die in prolonged pain.

- Because when they are out of the house they like to have something that they can order about.

- Because the dead game that can be seen is easy for the dog to retrieve.

- Because the wounded game that cannot be seen is difficult for men to pick up.

- Because the handsome retriever gives a finish almost equal to neat spats to a shooter's turn-out.

- Because it is much easier to gain credit for sportsmanship at a dog show than in the field and covert.

- Because there is a demand for stud services at remunerative fees.

POEM TO THE BLACK GROUSE

Good-morrow to thy sable beak
And glossy plumage, dark and sleek;
Thy crimson moon and azure eye,
Cock of the heath, so wildly sly.

Scottish poet Johanna Baillie (1762 to 1851)

NARROW ESCAPE

MUZZLE LOADERS could be fiendishly dangerous. Indeed, an incident that happened to Lord Walsingham in 1873 explains why the breech barrel gained popularity so rapidly.

Lord W was shooting partridges at his Norfolk estate Merton. He and a loader were positioned behind a hide made of hurdles.

The loader was kneeling down to load one gun, while Walsingham fired another above his head. At that moment a strong gust of wind blew a spark of unburnt powder back from the muzzle and ignited the powder that the loader was pouring into the second gun.

His lordship recalled, 'The metal powder flask, containing nearly ¾ lb of gunpowder exploded in the poor fellow's hand.'

Amazingly the man's hand was only lightly burned, although a huge hole was blown in the hurdle and bits of powder flask were found thirty yards away.

YORKSHIRE GOOSE PIE, 1791

TAKE A LARGE FAT GOOSE, split it down the back and take all the bone out; bone a turkey and two ducks the same way; season them with pepper and salt, with six woodcocks. Lay the goose down on a clean dish with the skin side down and lay the turkey into the goose with the skin down. Have ready a large hare, cleaned well; cut in pieces and put in the oven with 1 lb of butter, ¼ oz mace, beat fine; the same of white pepper, and salt to taste, till the meat will leave the bones, and scum off the gravy; pick the meat clean off and beat it in a marble mortar very fine with the butter you took off, and lay it on the turkey.

Take 24 lb of the finest flour, 6 lbs of butter, ½lb of fresh rendered suet, make the paste thick and raise the pie oval; roll out a lump of paste and cut it in vine leaves or what form you will; rub the pie with yolks of eggs and put your ornaments on the wall, then turn your hare, turkey and goose upside down and lay them on your pie with the ducks at each end and the woodcocks at the sides. Make your lid pretty thick and put it on. You may make flowers, or the shape of folds in the paste on the lid, and make a hole in the middle of the lid. The walls of the pie are to be 1½ in thicker than the lid. Rub it all over with the yolks of eggs and bind it round with three-fold paper and the same over the top. It will take four hours baking in a brown bread oven. When it comes out, melt 2 lb of butter in the gravy that came from the hare and pour it through a funnel into the goose. Close it well up and let it be eight or ten days before you cut into it. If you send it any distance, close up the hole in the middle with cold butter to prevent the air from getting in.

HOW MANY BEATERS CAN YOU SQUEEZE INTO A HORSEBOX?

Rules for transporting shoot beaters – as compiled by the British Association of Shooting and Conservation.

• Anyone riding as a passenger on any form of agricultural equipment should only do so in a properly constructed and secured seat. This does not necessarily rule out the use of straw bales but they must be secured.

• Where trailers are used the towing vehicle must be in good roadworthy condition, in particular steering, braking systems and tyres; secured, and coupled to the trailer in accordance with the Agriculture (Field Machinery) Regulations 1962.

• Trailers must also be in good condition, i.e., properly maintained tyres and braking which includes both parking and service brakes. The trailer floor must be in sound condition.

• Seating on trailers in addition to being securely fixed to the trailer bed must also be fitted with a backrest unless situated down the centre of the trailer. This should extend at least 400mm above the seat level. The front edge of the trailer must be fitted with a guardrail between 920mm and 1050mm above floor level. An intermediate rail and toe board is advisable. All other edges of the trailer must be fitted with a guardrail of similar specification (except where access is necessary).

• A safe means of access must be provided. This means a portable ladder, suitable for the purpose, securely held when access is required and carried in the trailer with the passengers. If fixed steps are used, the first step should not be more than 550mm from the ground. A secure handhold should be available to a height of 1050mm above the trailer floor. Where passengers are carried after dark, there must be a lighting system, which adequately illuminates the access, and the area of the trailer used by passengers, there must also be red taillights.

• A safe system of operation must be in place, the features of which should include:

> – a responsible person travelling on each trailer to assist passengers (not the driver). They must be able to contact the driver easily and the driver should be instructed not to move unless instructed by this person.
>
> – all passengers must remain seated whilst the vehicle is in motion.

Under the Road Vehicles (Construction & Use) Regulations 1986, as amended, Regulations 100 (1) states 'the number of passengers carried by such a vehicle or trailer, the manner in which any passenger is carried in or on such vehicles or trailer...shall at all times be such, that no danger is caused or is likely to be caused to any person in or on the vehicle or trailer or on a road.'

BASC say that beaters' transport is one area of shoot management, which does not receive enough attention. 'Quite often adequate arrangements are made for transporting the Guns (often their own four wheel drive vehicles) but on many shoots the beaters' transport, often a tractor and open trailer, is woefully inadequate and, on occasions, unsafe. Careful attention should be given to providing dedicated transport which is weatherproof, well constructed and fully serviceable on a shoot day.'

ON PARTRIDGES...

The fluttering coveys from the stubble rise,
And on swift wing divide the sounding skies,
The scattering lead pursues the certain sight,
And death in thunder overtakes their flight.

John Gay (1685 to 1732)

NOT SUCH A LARK

One of the more political English country sports writers was Robert Blakey (1795 to 1878), who produced several shooting 'n fishing books during the mid-nineteenth century.

Manchester-born Blakey, son of a Northumberland cotton factory worker, was a radical politician who tried to help the poor in his impoverished hometown of Morpeth. A keen shot and rabbit fur dealer, he was known as 'Robin Readypenny' because he always paid his suppliers on time and was never in debt.

Blakey became a friend of the radical journalist William Cobbett who encouraged him to take up left wing politics. Blakey was involved for many years in the agitation that led to the 1832 Reform Act. He made enough money from his early writing, mainly about philosophy, to buy a newspaper, the *Northern Liberator*, through which he lectured the middle classes on how it was their duty to help the poor.

By the 1850s Blakey was writing full time about country sports. And it is for these works that he is best known. His 1854 book *Angling And Shooting* was in print almost continuously for more than fifty years.

Blakey was passionate about field sports and believed that the working man should get into the countryside whenever he could. He wrote: 'A love of fieldsports generally, and of shooting in particular, takes us from the noise, and filth, and moral degradation incident to large towns. It places us in the midst of the cultivation of the soil – the real foundation of all national wealth and happiness. Everything connected with the wanderings of the sportsman is calculated to foster the best and noblest feelings of the soul, and to impart to the mind the most lofty and sublime ideas of universal nature.'

But Blakey was not keen on all forms of shooting. And he certainly had little time for the French. Here he describes a Gallic 'mode of amusement' known as 'twirling for larks.'

These birds are drawn to any given spot in considerable numbers by a singular contrivance called a mirror. This is a small machine, made of a piece of mahogany, shaped like a chapeau bras, and highly polished, with small bits of looking glass so as to reflect the sun's rays upwards. By pulling a string...the mirror twirls round, and the reflected light unaccountably attracts the larks, who hover over it, and become a mark for the shooting sportsman. There is often what the French call capital sport in this way. Sometimes six dozen of these birds are shot before breakfast. Ladies often partake of the amusement on a odd dry morning, not by shooting, but by watching the sport. Occasionally there are ten or a dozen parties out together, firing at a distance of five or six hundred yards, and by this device the larks are kept constantly on the wing. The most favourable mornings are when there is a gentle light frost, with little or no wind, and the sky clear. When cloudy the birds will not appear. To a bystander it would almost suggest that the larks themselves enjoyed their own destruction, for the fascination of the twirler is so strong as to rob them of the usual fruits of experience. After being fired at several times, they return to the twirler, and form again into groups above it.

Blakey concludes: 'We would advise young sportsmen to refrain from any such practices. The lark gladdens the heart of man . As Pope says, "Joy tunes his voice, joy elevates his wings.!" and we really do think that there ought not to be any sporting with his safety.'

DO YOU KNOW THE TYPE?

'The keeper who gives himself airs, loudly roars his commands in the field, and is generally noisy and talkative, is never to be trusted.'

Victorian shooting writer Sir Ralph Payne-Gallwey

ROYAL CONFUSION

THE PRINCE OF WALES, later Edward VII, was so obsessed by shooting that he devised 'Sandringham Time.'

In order to get in more shooting during the winter daylight hours, the 180 or so clocks across the Sandringham Estate were put forward by thirty minutes. Eddie's whimsy led to great confusion although it did have the advantage of assisting his wife Queen Alexandra, who was famous for her unpunctuality.

Sandringham Time continued after the death of Edward and through the reign of George V. However, while George lay dying in January 1936 several mistakes were made with doctors turning up late and medicine being administered at the wrong time.

Edward VIII partly attributed his father's death to this chaos. After coming to the throne he returned the clocks to the proper time.

✳ King Edward VII's enjoyment of shooting was based almost entirely on how many shots he could fire in a day. The King was an occasional guest of the Earl of Dartmouth at Patshull Park, outside Wolverhampton. Dartmouth found Edward's impatience so irksome that he employed two teams of beaters. As soon as one drive was finished another could start immediately, thereby keeping Eddie constantly amused.

✳ Edward VII experimented with putting down thousands of quail at Sandringham. An expensive mistake. The quail that were not shot migrated. And not one single bird returned. Under present legislation it is illegal to release quail for shooting in Britain since they are a non-native species.

ALL IN THE HEAD

'In shooting rabbits, think only of the head; there is no question of aiming, as there must be with a high pheasant: you swing your gun at them, thinking only of the head, and, shot through the head, the rabbit turns somersaults.'

From Elements of Shooting, *by Eric Parker, 1924*

THE OLD GAMEKEEPER

In actual years I understand
That he is turned of sixty-seven,
His rugged brows are seamed and tanned
With all the winds and suns of heaven;
Yet, though about his beard and hair
Old time has scattered snow in plenty,
He fronts you with a stalwart air,
As upright as a lad of twenty.

A patriarch this of sun and rod,
Of gaff and fly, of fur and feather,
Who upon fifty twelfths has trod
With Don and Rambler through the heather
Who as a round-eyed urchin stared
At older squires in strange apparel,
And can recall the present laird
A novice with a single barrel.

By Alfred Cochrane, 1898

ROYAL FIRSTS

IN THE FIRST ENTRY IN HIS GAME BOOK, twelve-year-old Prince Albert, later King George VI, noted, ' 23 December 1907, Wolferton Warren, Sandringham. Papa, David (his brother, later King Edward VIII) and myself. One pheasant, forty-seven rabbits. My first day's shooting. I used a single barrel muzzle loader with which Grandpapa, Uncle Eddy and Papa all started shooting. I shot three rabbits.'

The first entry in the game book of Prince Charles, aged eleven, stated that on 10 September 1960, he and four other guns shot twenty-eight grouse and twenty-two hares in Aberdeenshire. Charles commented, rather dully, and presumably because it was the sort of comment you were supposed to make in a game book: 'There was a strong SW wind blowing.'

WHICH WOOD?

A MUCH TOLD VICTORIAN SHOOTING STORY concerned a land owning peer, who, following a disaster of a drive where no birds appeared, lost his temper with his head keeper.

'Shall we find more birds in the next covert?'

'I hope so, my lord.'

'Hope, sir!' roared the peer. 'Do you think I give you £100 a year to hope?' Pointing at a wood, his lordship yelled, 'Now get your beaters over there and find us some pheasants.'

'Surely your lordship means this wood,' said the trembling keeper, pointing at closer covert.

'No, I mean that wood. Now get going.'

The beaters pushed the wood through. Not a single bird appeared.

The keeper was summoned. 'You're sacked,' said the peer.

'But it wasn't your wood,' whimpered the miserable keeper. 'It belongs to your neighbour Lord Y…and he shot it yesterday.'

WHY KEEPERS SHOULDN'T SHOOT FOXES…

'The sport which foxes afford, the benefit of fox-hunting, socially and pecuniarily, to every neighbourhood where a pack of fox-hounds exists, the amusement afforded thereby to all classes of society, and the churlishness of putting a check to it for the purpose of adding slightly to the pleasure of the owner of the coverts they frequent and a mere handful of his friends, are all considerations which should induce a gamekeeper to pause long and often 'ere he allow the fox to be included in the list of vermin. Besides all this, the mischief foxes do is very greatly exaggerated. Where rabbits abound they will molest little else, and a great head of game can be killed in coverts which are full of foxes if the keeper really understand his business.'

From Shooting Field And Covert, *by the Hon. Gerald Lascelles,*
Badminton Library, 1885

GROUSE ESSENTIALS

The Oakleigh Shooting Code, a splendid 1838 manual that was essential reading for all nineteenth century sportsmen, lists the items that the grouse-shooting gent should take with him on the moor:

- dogs
- gun
- gun-rod, olive oil and linen-cloth (for cleaning gun)
- powder-flask
- canister of gun powder
- shot belt
- canister of shot
- several pairs of woollen stockings
- boots or strong shoes and gaiters
- dark coloured shooting suit
- copper caps and box
- wadding and punch for cutting wadding
- screw driver and spring cramp
- shoe oil
- spare boot straps
- spare collars
- cord for tying up dog
- dog whistle
- dog whip
- pocket knife
- pocket comb (to maintain smart appearance at all times)
- string for tying up game
- hampers in which to pack grouse
- sealing wax and seal for labelling birds
- game certificate
- letter of permission to show gamekeepers
- pedometer
- compass
- sandwiches, cigars, soda powders, prometheans (small glass tubes of sulphuric acid which when broken produce fire, forerunner of the match)
- telescope (to view the scenery)
- dram-flask

- brandy (presumably to give you strength to carry all this clobber)

The author adds rather unhelpfully, 'Half these things may be dispensed with.'

THREE VIEWS ON LUNCH

Augustus Grimble, from *Shooting and Salmon Fishing and Highland Sport*, 1902:

As to shooting lunches, we have seen too much provided...champagne, with hot substantial solids capped with cake, old cognac, and cigars, is not calculated to improve anyone's shooting; but all the same it is preferable to cold tea with dry biscuits, which fare we once saw five guns asked to sit down to, at a white hare drive in November, at an altitude of two thousand feet above sea level! We consider champagne is fatal to good marksmanship or stout walking, and have several times felt (only just to see if it really was the case) how it spoils the eye, and have witnessed the same effect on many others. We especially remember the occasion of a ptarmigan day early in September on a hill top which was absolutely springless, so thus it happened that two bottles of champagne were put into the panniers, with beer for the men, to save the waste of time in descending and remounting the steep hill to find a spring for luncheon. Now, two bottles between three was not a very extravagant allowance after five hours' hard walking in a hot sun… and yet on one of the party his share had the effect of causing him, an old deer stalker, to mistake mutton for venison on a sky line not a quarter of a mile distant, while for about half an hour after lunch we all three shot very badly; so beware champagne in the field is our advice.

J. J Manley, from *Notes on Game and Game Shooting*, 1880:

Work on quietly but perseveringly till luncheon, and let the spot for this important crisis of the day be well chosen. Let it be a under a hedge, but a well considered and well carried affair. It is an utter mistake to imagine that cold viands are most appropriate for heated and jaded frames. Hot soups, stews, hashes, or pies and hot potatoes – they will keep hot for hours wrapped in flannel – are most palatable and refreshing in hot weather, on the same principle that hot curry is eaten in India and hot soup at balls. Sandwiches and cold meat fall very flat and insipid on the palate when you are hot and exhausted. They are stale and unprofitable. This may not be the generally accepted law, but I maintain it is the true one. As to your drink, that is an entirely different matter. Let that be as cold as possible. A small iceberg enwrapped in flannel is a most enjoyable adjunct to the partridge shooting lunch. Drink champagnes, claret, hock, or any other light wines, with or

without soda water, but, as a rule, eschew beer, sherry, and spirits, and by the by, if your shooting lies over a dry land where no water is, do not forget to have some brought for the poor dogs, who will enjoy it as much as you will the best iced drink at your command. Do not be in a hurry with your lunch – nor afterwards. Take a cigar, lie on your back, stretch your legs, with your heels up if possible, after the sensible American fashion. Even a siesta – a short one, of course – in my opinion is not only allowable but advisable in some cases. A full hour or an hour and a half devoted to luncheon is not time lost, to say nothing of the agreeable way of spending it. There is plenty of time left before sundown to make a good bag, and after your midday rest you will resume your sport like giants refreshed.

Sir Joseph Nickerson, *from* A Shooting Man's Creed,
Swan Hill Press, 2006:

'Avoid gossiping about it if you happen to invite a cabinet minister to your shoot. Make sure his bodyguards, if he has them, get a decent lunch as well as the rest of the Guns.'

ANTI-POACHER DEVICE

One of the most unusual weapons produced by an English gun maker was Thomas Horsley's alarm gun.

Horsley was a Yorkshire gunsmith who in the 1870s found a gap in the market for anti-poacher devices. Up to now keepers had simply nailed an old gun (probably confiscated from a poacher) to a tree and attached a tripwire. But Horsley was determined to custom build a device.

The Horsley alarm gun was a massive mushroom-shaped contraption weighing 7.5 kg. When a trip wire was released the top crashed onto the pin of a 12-bore pinfire cartridge. Unlike todays's harmless alarm devices which fire blanks, the Horsley was specifically designed to fire a live cartridge along the line of the trip wire aimed at the poacher's legs.

However, the short 7.5 cm barrel would have been unlikely to create anything more than a cloud of smoke and some low velocity shot that would have stung rather than wound.

It is unknown if any poachers were killed by this contraption but plenty were frightened. In a letter to *The Field* in 1887 a correspondent wrote: 'I can speak highly of such guns. Living, as I do, near a large town, I have found them most effective. I remember some three or four years ago, being out one night, when we heard one of our guns go off about a mile away. We ran to it…the fraternity had evidently started to set their nets, come across the wire, and made off without daring to go back for their bags. Poachers, as a rule, are an arrant lot of cowards; and I verily believe if they know a wood is well set with alarm guns they will not trouble it.'

THE BASC IDEAL

'That all who shoot in Britain conduct themselves according to the law and to the highest standards of safety, sportsmanship and courtesy, with full respect for their quarry and a practical interest in wildlife conservation and in the countryside. Never guess at what the Law allows. If in doubt, contact BASC or your local police firearms licensing department.'

From the British Association of Conservation and Shooting handbook

TASTES BETTER THAN IT READS

FIFTEENTH CENTURY ENGLISH RECIPE FOR COOKING SMALL GAME BIRDS:

Take a Sorcell (sarcelle, a small duck) or a tele (teal), and breke his necke, and pul him dry, And draw him as a chekon, and kutte off his fete and wings by the body and the nekke, and roste him, and reise his winges and his legges as a heron, if he be a Sorcell; And no sauce but salt.

Take a wodecok, and sle him as the plouer; pul him dry, or elles breke his bakke, And lete the sculle be hole; drawe him, And kutte of his winges by the body, and turne vp the legges as thou doest of a crane; put his bill thorgh bothe his thighes; roste him, And reise his legges And his winges, as thou doest of all maner of other clouen fote fowle.

Take a Snyte (snipe), and sle him as thou doest a wodecok; pulle him, late his necke be hole, save the wesing; put the bill in the shulder, and folde the legges as a Crane; roste him, And dight him as the Wodecok.

OLDEST GUNS

THE WORLD'S OLDEST GUN MAKER is Beretta, and they are also one of the planet's oldest industrial operations. The company was founded in the 1520s in the town of Gardone in northern Italy by Bartolomeo Beretta. His son and grandchildren rapidly took the business forward and towards the end of the sixteenth century Beretta were making up to three hundred guns per day using assembly line methods. By the early twentieth century the company was world renowned. So prominent was Beretta in Gardone that the town even featured the Beretta Hotel where visitors to the factory could stay.

HALF THE TIME AND HALF THE DISCOMFORT

THE INVENTION OF THE MOTOR CAR caused great excitement in the shooting world. By the turn of the twentieth century cars were to be found taking guns across fields and up to moors in the same way that a horse and carriage had done in the past.

One of the greatest fans of the car was a Member of Parliament called the Hon. John Scott-Montagu – the father of the present Lord Montagu of Beaulieu who established the National Motor Museum in his memory.

In 1903 Scott-Montagu wrote an article for *Country Life* about motorised shooting. The piece included a picture of him and fellow Guns aboard a car at a shoot in Hampshire. 'The motor car is especially adaptable for shooting expeditions,' the Hon. John raved. 'After shooting, the long drive home in a carriage, especially if it has been a wet day, is undeniably most tiresome and uncomfortable. In a motor, however, whatever distance you have to go can be accomplished in half the time and with half the discomfort.'

The car was particularly good for August duck flighting. 'Ducks at that time of the year do not begin to flight properly before 7.30 to 8. This means that for the return journey a motor car is a much more speedy and comfortable means of reaching a late dinner or supper than an ordinary carriage. There is also the point that on rainy and windy nights the motor car can wait close by and not catch cold, as a pair of horses would do. The driver also is free – not being required to watch the motor car, as in the case of an ordinary vehicle – and he can leave his car and help in carrying cartridges, marking down wounded birds, or making himself generally useful.'

Up north the car was essential kit for grouse shooting. 'There are many little patches of moor suitable for men of moderate means which have no house or lodge attached, and these smaller moors are now accessible by means of the motor car.'

The car was also the 'best hill-climber known,' particularly when it has 'a small enough sprocket wheel when the proportion of engine power to diameter of wheel has been so adjusted as to give hill-climbing qualities.'

However, Scott-Montagu issued two warnings. The first concerned dogs. 'Dogs in general have not yet learnt to get out of the way of a car, therefore motormen should approach at a very slow speed, otherwise a valuable retriever may be seriously hurt.'

The second concerned hunting. 'I will not dilate here on the vexed question as to whether in a hunting county motor cars are or are not desirable. Hunting involves the cult of the horse, and in Rome it is advisable to do what Rome likes…'

❋ Nearly forty years later the motor car was still causing consternation in shooting circles. Here is a marvellous rant from field sports writer Julian Tennyson in his 1938 book *Rough Shooting*: As often or not the poacher of today is – oh sacrilege – a townsman who works from a car, careering about the land and shooting everything indiscriminately without leaving his seat. By night he makes use of his headlights to dazzle his victims, dashing away in a whirl of dust and laughter, and sometimes such poaching is done by whole fleets of fast cars. O sorry plight, to think that the wary otter, that outlaw of the woods and fields, should be succeeded by such an ignorant bandit! It seems that a motor poacher can belong to any walk of life. Company directors, undergraduates, bank clerks, factory hands, small provincial townsmen – all of these have been caught in the last fifteen years. Perhaps the day will come when poaching will be done by machine gun from an aeroplane.

TYPES OF SHOT

Alternatives to lead for when the eco crowd manage to ban lead completely:

Steel:
Made from short lengths of soft iron wire which are mechanically rounded. The drawback is that the density of steel is lower than lead so it needs a higher powder charge. Secondly, it is much harder than lead which means it can scratch the barrels of your beloved Purdey. Should never be used in barrels tighter than half choke. Thirdly, lumps of iron in a cooked bird could play havoc with your teeth. And *never* put steel in a Damascus barrel.

Tin:
Much more expensive than steel but softer, like lead.

Bismuth:
Even more expensive and a little less dense than lead. Said not to have the killing power of lead but acceptable except for the price.

Tungsten matrix:
The Rolls-Royce of shot, most expensive of them all. Has virtually the same density as lead so virtually lead's equal. You may have to sell your Purdey to pay for it.

Bow and arrow:
Probably the only thing we will eventually be allowed.

ENOUGH TO MAKE YOU SEE ORANGE

The most mind-boggling game laws in America concern whether or not it is compulsory to wear da-glo orange vests. The idea is that if you are dressed in 'hunter orange' safety blaze you are less likely to be shot by a fellow hunter. However, rather than having a comprehensive 'orange' policy across America, each state has its own rules. And very confusing they are too...

Alabama: all hunters during deer season must wear a vest or cap with at least 144 square inches of solid orange, visible from all sides. Deer hunters in tree stands elevated more than twelve feet from the ground need not wear orange, except when traveling to and from tree stands. Only Hunter Orange, Blaze Orange or Ten Mile cloth is legal. (Exception: waterfowl, turkey and dove hunters and those hunting legally designated species during legal night time hours.)

Alaska, Arizona, California, Idaho, Nevada, New Hampshire, New Mexico, New York, Oregon, Vermont: orange strongly recommended but not compulsory.

Arkansas: unlawful to hunt any wildlife, or to accompany or assist anyone in hunting wildlife, during a gun or muzzle loading deer season without wearing an outer garment above the waistline, of daylight fluorescent blaze orange (hunter orange) within the color range of 595nm (hunter safety green) totaling at least 400 square inches, and a fluorescent blaze orange or fluorescent chartreuse head garment must be visibly worn on the head.

Colorado: hunters must wear at least 500 square inches of solid daylight fluorescent orange material in an outer garment above the waist, part of which must be a hat or head covering visible from all directions while hunting deer, elk or antelope during any muzzle loading or rifle seasons. Bow hunters are not required to wear orange during archery only seasons.

Connecticut: 1 September to last day of February you must wear at least 400 square inches of fluorescent orange clothing above the waist visible from all sides. Does not apply to archery deer hunting; on private lands during the private land muzzle loader season; on private lands in Deer Management Zones 11 and 12 during the firearms deer seasons when hunting from an elevated tree stand at least 10 feet from the ground (orange is required when walking to and from the stand); to archery and firearms turkey hunting; to waterfowl hunters hunting from blinds or a stationary position; to hunting raccoon and opossum from one half hour after sunset to one half hour before sunrise; or to deer hunting by a landowner on his own property. Phew!

Delaware, Louisiana, Illinois, Montana, Nebraska, North Dakota, Oklahoma, Utah, Washington, West Virginia : during deer season hunters must display on head, chest and back not less than 400 square inches of orange. Illinois exception: you only have to wear an orange hat when shooting upland game such as pheasant, rabbit, quail or partridge. Oklahoma exception: orange not compulsory for waterfowl, crow, or crane hunters, and those hunting fur bearing animals at night. Utah exception: you are not required to wear hunter orange material during an archery, muzzle loader, or bighorn sheep hunt, unless a centerfire rifle hunt is in progress in the same area.

Florida, Georgia, Massachusetts, Mississippi, Tennessee : during deer, (and bear and feral hog season in Georgia) hunters must display on head, chest and back not less than 500 square inches of orange. Massachusetts exception: raccoon hunters at night. Tennessee exception: turkey hunters and those hunting on their own property.

Hawaii, Kentucky, Michigan, Minnesota, Missouri, North Carolina, Ohio, South Carolina, South Dakota, Wyoming: unspecified amount of orange compulsory for all hunters.

Indiana and Iowa: deer, rabbit, squirrel, grouse, pheasant, and quail hunters must wear at least one orange garment.

Kansas: each individual hunting deer or elk and each individual assisting an individual hunting deer or elk, shall wear orange clothing having a predominant lightwave length of 595–605 nanometers; The bright orange color shall be worn as follows: 1) a hat with the exterior of not less than 50 per cent of the bright orange color, an equal portion of which is visible from all directions; 2) a minimum of 100 square inches of the bright orange color on the front of the torso; and 3) a minimum of 100 square inches of the bright orange color on the back of the torso.

Maine: anyone who hunts with a firearm during any open firearm season on deer is required to wear two articles of solid colored fluorescent orange which is visible from all sides. One article must be a hat.

Maryland: all hunters and those accompanying them must wear either: 1) a cap of solid daylight fluorescent orange color; 2) a vest or jacket containing back and front panels of at least 250 square inches of solid daylight fluorescent orange color. Exception: hunters of wetland game birds, fur bearing mammals, doves, crows, wild turkeys, bow hunters during archery season only, falconers, and unlicenced hunters on their own property. Double phew!

New Jersey: all hunters with firearms for deer, rabbit, hare, squirrel, fox or game birds must wear an orange cap or other garment with at least 200 square inches of orange visible from all sides. (Exception: waterfowl, wild turkey and bow hunters.)

Pennsylvania: hunters must wear at least 250 square inches of hunter orange material on the head, chest and back combined. Spring turkey hunters must wear a minimum of 100 square inches of hunter orange on the head or back and chest while moving from one location to another. Groundhog hunters must wear 100 square inches of hunter orange on the head. Exceptions: waterfowl, mourning dove, crow, flintlock deer season and archery season hunters except as specified. Triple phew!

Rhode Island: solid daylight flourescent orange is required statewide, and must be worn above the waist and be visible in all directions. Examples which meet the orange requirements are a hat that covers 200 sq. in. or a combination of hat and vest covering 500 sq. in. The following orange requirements apply: 200 sq. in. by small game hunters during the small game season; 200 sq. in. by muzzle loader hunters during the muzzle loader season; 200 sq. in. by archers when traveling to/from stands during muzzle loading season; 500 sq. in. by all hunters (including archers) and all Management Area users during shotgun deer season. Exemptions: waterfowl hunters while hunting from a boat or blind, over water or field, when done in conjunction with decoys; Crow hunters, when hunting over decoys; Turkey hunters; First segment dove hunters. In addition to above requirements, all other users (hikers, bicyclists, horseback riders, etc.) of State Management Areas are required to wear 200 sq. in. of solid daylight flourescent orange from the third Saturday in October to the last day of February annually, and during the established mourning dove season and wild turkey season. Quadruple phew!

Texas: hunters must wear a minimum of 144 square inches of orange.

Virginia: hunters must wear at least 100 square inches of orange.

Wisconsin: all hunters must have orange on 50 per cent of their outer garments above the waist.

✳ In Virginia the law is hopelessly confusing. Most hunters, no matter what they're after have to wear at least an orange cap. However, blaze orange is not required of people going wildfowling, nor those participating in field trials or using black powder. Wildfowling, field trials and muzzle-loading must be particularly dangerous pursuits in Virginia. Either that or the shooting folk are colourblind. In 2006 hunting fatalities in the state doubled from four to eight.

Orange garb has been a great success up in New Hampshire where the average annual number of hunting deaths has dropped from twenty-one in the 1960s to less than five in 2007. Legislators see this as a remarkable accomplishment when you consider that more than 63,000 deer hunters take to the field during the twenty-six day season. 'Wearing hunter orange has definitely been shown to decrease hunting incidents across the country,' said Tom Flynn, a Hunter Education Coordinator for the state's Fish and Game Department. 'It's especially important for hunters, because the overwhelming majority of hunting related incidents involve members of the same hunting party, not non-hunters. Along with wearing blaze orange, the top safety rules for hunters are controlling the muzzle of your gun at all times and positively identifying your target and what's beyond 100 per cent of the time.' Author's comment: Would it not be a lot simpler – and safer – if American hunters were taught not to shoot if they can't be sure where the shot or bullet is going to end up? Or to take the words of Mark Beaufoy:

> 'Calm and steady always be;
> Never shoot where you can't see'

DEER IN SHADES

With a brochure featuring a deer in dark glasses, an American firm have developed an orange da-glo material that animals can't see. The product is proving a great success in US states where it is compulsory for hunters to wear an orange blaze safety vest – to avoid being shot themselves.

The problem with standard orange vests is that Bambi can see you a mile off. But this material, produced by a company called Covert Orange, looks nothing more alarming than a bluey-grey to your average elk. Ophthalmology researcher Dr Lincoln Johnson says, 'Colour vision in animals, including humans, depends upon the number and type of colour sensitive cells in the eye. Human eyes have three types of colour sensitive cells. Deer and other game animals are sensitive to only two colours, blue and yellow. As a result, a human and a deer perceive the colour of the same object differently.'

Covert Orange utilises a combination of high intensity UV chemical that makes deer think it is much duller than it is. And in spite of this tremendous advantage to the hunter, the material is still highly visible to fellow hunters.

A PLEA FOR EQUALITY

A PLEA FOR EQUALITY from the website of London's top shooting 'n' fishing outfitters, Farlow's of Pall Mall:

Too often by the time a woman has abandoned the garish pink of her Barbie doll for the more sombre tones of a Barbour, her role in the shooting field has been designated. And since she won't have had the benefit of trying out Dad's old .410 and progressing to a 20-bore, in the way her male counterpart may have done, her position will, naturally, be of a more menial nature. She may be allowed to do a spot of beating, carry the cartridge bag or prepare the traditional shoot lunch – and let me emphasise there is nothing wrong with these tasks if that's what you choose to do. But what chances are there for the woman who wants to bag her own pheasant?

Physically there is no reason at all why women should not be as proficient at shooting as men. Contrary to popular belief, they are no more recoil-shy than men nor any more susceptible to its cumulative effect. Given a well-fitted stock of the correct length, with a good bit of cast at the toe, a woman can absorb as much recoil as anyone, as our top lady clay Shots prove time and again. The reason why women have not traditionally taken up shooting stems not from physical reasons, but purely sociological ones. When Queen Victoria declared 'only fast women shoot' she did an immense disservice to the sport. Where previously there was no such taboo, suddenly it wasn't 'the done thing' for a woman to be seen in the shooting line and it has taken decades to dispel the image of the lady Gun having somewhat loose morals. While Annie Oakley was wowing American audiences with her trick shooting and proving that she was equally skilled at shooting live pigeon as she was at hitting clay targets, over here women abandoned all notions of picking up a gun and it was left to the menfolk to bag a rabbit for supper. But today there are no such restrictions and game shooting has never been more accessible and affordable.

TRICKY SEALS

UNTIL THE MID-NINETEENTH CENTURY the sportsman's badge of honour was earned by shooting and picking a stag, a golden eagle...and a seal.

The stag and the eagle were easy. Seals were a different matter entirely. They were easy to kill but difficult to bag. A seal had be shot dead instantly or otherwise it would struggle into the water and sink. Therefore you had to approach it carefully while it was basking on rocks or sand. Since this generally meant shooting from a bobbing boat the chances of a single killing shot were small.

A PREFERABLE THING TO GLORY

SIR THOMAS BUXTON was a British philanthropist and politician who, in 1822, succeeded William Wilberforce as leader of the campaign in the House of Commons for the abolition of slavery.

Buxton became famous for his tireless campaigning. The newspapers wrote him up as one of the greatest Englishmen ever. But in private he had little time for fame and preferred to take himself off shooting.

Buxton was a first class shot and often skived off official duties in order to pursue his hobby. Three years after taking over from Wilberforce, Buxton wrote to a friend , 'I shall speak as well as I can in the House of Commons for usefulness, but not for fame, my serious opinion being that good woodcock shooting is a preferable thing to glory.'

Public life took its toll and towards the end of his life Buxton complained of a great weariness. His family motto was 'Whatever thy hand findest to do, do it with thy might.' Buxton wrote to his brother Edward in 1840: 'I do not think my motto and I square well together nowadays. I have no might, nor energy, nor pluck, nor anything of that sort, and this listlessness reaches even to my two pet pursuits – negroes and partridges.'

RURAL TRICKS

Amongst the more unusual field sports is a pastime called Hunting For Bambi. As you might imagine, with a name like that such a sport can only be found in America, or rather in the environs of rural Las Vegas.

The idea is that you pay up to $10,000 to shoot naked women with paint ball guns and get a video to take home to show your friends.

A millionaire participant named George explains it thus: 'I'm from New York. What am I gonna hunt? Squirrels? Cats? Dogs? I don' think so. I've never been hunting before. Now I can put on camo, grab a rifle and pull the trigger. And get a pretty girl in the sights.'

The girls are mostly moonlighting lapdancers. Dressed only in tennis shoes and eye goggles, they are paid considerably more than in a Las Vegas club. They earn $2,500 if they don't get hit, and $1,000 if they do. 'You try very hard to hide,' a girl called Nicole says.

However, there is a significant health and safety issue in that apart from goggles they are not allowed to wear protective gear. Organiser Michael Burdick says 'The main goal is to be as true to nature as possible. I don't go deer hunting and see a deer with a football helmet on so I don't want to see one on my girl either.'

Hunting For Bambi has not gone down well with the bunny huggers. Indeed, it has caused an uproar across America with outrage from women's groups and traditional paint-ballers alike. Las Vegas city council have joined the affray threatening to close down the hunts because Burdick does not have a licence for a 'sexually oriented business.' Mayor Oscar Goodman says, 'We're gonna stop it. Any guy that's gonna pay $10,000 to shoot ping pong balls at a naked woman has gotta be an idiot.'

ADDRESSING THE RAIN

A guest of Sir Timothy Eden, brother of former prime minister Anthony, came down early to breakfast on the morning of a big grouse day at Sir Timothy's Scottish estate, to find his host at the dining room window shaking his fist at the pouring rain and saying 'Oh, God, how like you!'

THE SETTER AT WORK

When autumn smiles, all beauteous in decay,
And paints each chequered grove with various hues,
My setter ranges in the new shorn fields,
His nose in air erect; from ridge to ridge,
Panting, he bounds, his quartered ground divides
In equal intervals, nor careless leaves one inch untried.
At length the tainted gale
His nostrils wide inhale, quick joy elates
His beating heart, which, awed by discipline severe,
He dares not own, but cautious creeps low-cowering, step by step;
At last attains his proper distance, there he stops at once,
And points with his instructive nose upon the trembling prey.
On wings of wind and upborne
The floating net unfolded flies; then drops,
And the poor fluttering captives rise in vain.

William Somerville (1675 to 1742)

KEEP LOW PROFILE

'When staying in a town, take care not to let everyone know where you shoot by pompously riding through it with a display of guns and dogs. Either send on the latter in the dark, or take them closely shut up in your dog-cart. If driving, cover your shooting dress with a mackintosh or box-coat. If on horseback, ride out of town on some road diametrically opposite to where your sport lies, and then double back again on the other roads, or by crossing the country. If you return by daylight, enter the town…in the most quiet and private manner, otherwise you will soon have your beat worked by every townsman who can muster a gun and a dog.'

From Instructions to Young Sportsmen, *by Col. Peter Hawker, 1814*

SUBURBAN GROUSE

As late as 1880 they were shooting black grouse off corn stubble in parts of Berkshire, including Ascot Heath. More grouse could be found on the Merstham Hills in Surrey in what is now deepest suburbia.

A CURIOUS AND INTERESTING PHENOMENON

'Towering is one of those curious and interesting phenomena which, though singular to behold, is puzzling alike to the sportsman and naturalist. It is more frequently met with in partridge shooting than in any other sport. Towering is the last gasp or death struggle of a dying bird when mortally wounded, though the precise nature and locality of the wound, which affects the bird so remarkably as to incite it to such an extraordinary and beautiful effort in its dying moments, has never been ascertained with sufficient certainty to satisfy the curious inquirer.

'It has often been the subject of discussion and speculation among sportsmen and naturalists, as to what it is that causes a bird to tower; or rather, in what particular part the bird receives its mortal wound. Or rather, in what particular part the bird receives its mortal wound so as to cause it to perform so pretty an evolution in the air. Some say it only occurs when the bird receives a shot in the head or brain; others affirm that it arises from a shot going through the liver; others from a wound in the spine; but without asserting any thing positive upon so truly scientific an inquiry, I am disposed to think it arises from a mortal wound in one of the main arteries of the heart.'

From The Dead Shot, *by 'Marksman', 1860*

RABBIT SHOOTING

More difficult than hares to hit,
They frequently appear to flit
Like shadows past one – good, indeed,
Is then the aim that bids them bleed.
If you would see them nicely stopped
In the thick wood, you must adopt
Snap shooting, for you'll seldom there
Have time to take them full and fair;
E'en lost to view, advance your gun
Quickly to where you *think* they run:
Regard not grass, nor brush, nor briar,
Though each and all that instant fire.
Bang! It's well - you saw him not
And yet you've killed him on the spot.

Victorian poem, by W. Watt

HOW TO BE TOP DOG

Owners of pampered pooches, take note!

When you let your dog sleep on your bed you are allowing him to contest your position as leader. No dog pack leader would allow its space to be occupied by an underling. Therefore your dog sees you as a weak leader who could do with replacing. This leads to aggression problems.

When you let your dog pull on the lead, he is *your* leader.

When your dog comes up to you with a ball and drops it at your feet asking you to throw it for him, he is showing dominance by initiating play. If you throw it for him you are therefore following *his* orders.

When you give your dog his meals before yours, you are telling him he's the boss. Leader eats first, underlings get the scraps. That is dog instinct.

The dog that guards the home and growls at visitors is taking on the role of pack leader, deciding who is a threat and who is not.

From Dogs Misbehaving, *by Martin J. Scott and Gael Mariani, Kenilworth Press, 2001*

RESPECT YOUR QUARRY

'Another ritual, and one of which I fully approved, was the laying out of the day's bag on the lawn in front of the big house. Too many shoots treat the birds they shoot with little or no respect. I hate to see pheasants tossed into the back of a Land Rover and trampled by the Guns' boots and dogs' paws. Pheasant, grouse, partridge, snipe, woodcock, mallard, teal, pigeon or rabbit: they are all beautiful creatures in their respective ways and deserve better than to be thrown in a heap and left to sweat on the floor of a vehicle. There is a practical side to all this as well. A pheasant that is dumped in a heap with a dozen others and left to sweat for three or four hours...will be deteriorating even before you collect your brace at the end of the day. Hang it for a week or so and the odds are that it will be green and stinking by the time you come to dress it out. But hang that same bird in a dry game-cart where the air can cool it as soon as it has been picked, and it will be...very tasty a week or even a fortnight hence. And the end product of all the effort that goes into shooting is, after all, a roast pheasant on your dinner plate.'

From The Small Shoot, *by David Hudson, Swan Hill Press, 2003*

THE PARTRIDGE AND THE FOWLER

A fowler was about to kill a partridge he had just caught. The partridge begged earnestly for his life. 'Pray, master, permit me to live and I will entice many partridges to you in recompense for your mercy to me.'

The fowler replied, 'I shall now with less scruple take your life, because you are willing to save it at the cost of betraying your friends and relations.'

Aesop's Fable, circa 600 BC

THE FIRST DRIVE

We wait behind the blackthorn hedge,
The beaters' sow advance;
Gold sedges hold the sun in pledge,
A finch's gold wings glance;
Faint-calling partridges afar...
My son, in briefest words,
The roots beyond the sare
Fair chock-a-block with birds.

Ah, here they come! The first lot springs
Aloft and skims adown
The stubble with a flick of wings,
Quick swerving, trim and brown;
Now, ere they cross the space between,
Now, Diana, grant me this, That where I hit, I kill 'em clean,
That when I miss, I miss.

Extract from The First Drive, *by Patrick Chalmers*

ADVICE FOR THE GLORIOUS TWELFTH

Over-eager grouse shots should heed this advice from author John Colquhoun, writing in his book *The Moor And The Loch*, 1841: 'Most young shots are not content unless they are upon the moor by peep of day on the long-anticipated 12th of August – and what is the result? They have found and disturbed most of the packs before they have well fed, and one half will rise out of distance and fly away unbroken. Had the moor been left quiet till eight or nine o'clock, fair double shots might have been obtained at almost every pack... My advice, therefore, to the young grouse-shooter, is always to wait till the birds have done feeding.'

PROOF LAWS

The problem with the earliest guns was that they had an unfortunate tendency to explode due to bad workmanship. The number of horrible accidents suffered at the hands of dodgy firearms eventually led to the proof laws.

Nobody can be sure when it first became compulsory to proof firearms in England. But by the beginning of the seventeenth century gun makers were privately proofing their own barrels. Rather than wanting to protect the public, this had more to do with hard commercial practice in that it was a way of guaranteeing their products in order to achieve better sales. But still the rogue gunsmiths continued to knock out inferior barrels.

The first proof law was passed in 1672 when the London Company of Gunmakers (est. 1637) was granted a charter giving them the power to search for badly made guns in workshops within a ten mile radius of London. A 'proof' house was established in London. Then, as now, guns were tested for integrity by using a larger load than they would be subjected to in normal service. If a gun stood up to this punishment with no weakness, proof marks were stamped on the barrel to prove it was serviceable and would not cause its user injury. The marks, which are still used today, covered calibre, type and quantity of propellant charge, choking of the barrels and suitability of the weapon for shot or solid ball.

The next development in proofing was the establishment of The Birmingham Gun Barrel Proof House in 1813 at the request the Birmingham gun trade. And eventually the Gun Barrel Proof Acts 1868-1989 made it an offence to sell, offer for sale, transfer, export or pawn an unproofed firearm. Today the Birmingham Proof House still tests ammunition and investigates firearm accidents. Gun dealers can be fined up to £5,000 for selling an unproofed or out of proof firearm and there are further severe penalties for tampering with or forging a proof mark.

Currently proof law is covered by the Gun Barrel Proof Acts 1868, 1950 and 1978. Arms may be submitted for proof or reproof direct to either of the London or Birmingham proof houses. Proof regulations require that shotgun barrels 'shall be smooth and that insides shall be clean.' Pitting should be removed so far as is practicable, bulges knocked down and dents raised. Actions should be in good, safe working order and tight on the face to resist the increased strain of proof pressure. Since stocks are not designed to withstand the heavy recoil of proof, the wood should be removed before testing. If a gun is rejected, it may be repaired and resubmitted. But if it is impossible to repair, the proofer will deface the existing proof marks and will recommend that the gun be deactivated, thus ensuring that it can never be used again.

The proof houses also offer a service to home cartridge loaders to test their ammunition to ensure correct breech pressures and velocities. Home loaders are not legally bound to do this on the basis that their products cannot be legally sold. Experience of the proof houses shows that many home loaders haven't a clue what they are doing and frequently blow themselves up by using overcharged cartridges.

WHAT IS YOUR MOST DIFFICULT SHOT?

The thoughts of some of the most elegant shots in Britain were encapsulated in an early Edwardian edition of a periodical called *Badminton Magazine*. The question was: what sort of bird presents the most difficult shot?

Lord Ripon: A high pheasant coming down wind with a drop and a curl.

Lord Walsingham: A bird which comes straight over your head at a moderate height, and which for some reason (e.g. empty gun, thick wood ahead) cannot be shot when approaching and must be shot behind following a quick turn which means you instinctively try to shoot under it.

Marquess of Granby: A genuinely 'tall' pheasant, sailing with motionless wings, curling and possibly dropping as well.

Prince Victor Duleep Singh (son of the famous Maharajah): A high dropping pheasant with a wind behind and wings practically motionless.

Lord Westbury: Cock pheasant dropping with out-stretched wings and curling away.

Lord Ashburton: A pheasant, thirty-five to forty yards away, crossing and dropping with motionless wings.

Hon. Sir Harry Stonor (bachelor who served in five Royal households): A high cock pheasant flying down the line of guns with wings outstretched and apparently motionless.

Mr Reginald Rimington-Wilson: Really high pheasants in a wind and with a curl.

Note: for all the above a high pheasant was the most difficult bird, way ahead of the partridge and the grouse.

FROM PARTRIDGES TO PARSONS

The Gentleman's Magazine of January 1828 reported the obituary of Sir William Willoughby Wolstan Dixie Bt. who died of natural causes aged sixty-five at his family seat of Bosworth Hall, Leicestershire, close to the site of the Battle of Bosworth Field.

Sir William had in his youth been a keen shooting man. That was until his troubled genes overtook him and he began to seek quarry other than the usual pheasant and partridge.

The obituary writer explained, 'The deceased Baronet was subject to a degree of insanity with which the family has been long afflicted.'

Rather inconveniently, Sir William developed a dislike to men of the cloth and became known in the locale for taking potshots at parsons.

'In 1825 he made himself conspicuous by shooting from his windows at two clergymen who were passing. He was confined to Leicester gaol to wait trial.' Luckily the clerics decided not to press charges and Sir William was released.

Sir William's ancestor the fourth baronet, also called Sir Wolstan (1700-1767), was not much saner and raised eyebrows by giving his butler the job of headmaster of the local grammar school.

Sir Wolstan Snr. became a minor celebrity following a confrontation with a waggoner. The man was driving along a public road through Bosworth Park when Sir Wolstan halted him, pulled him from the cart, and gave him a good thrashing.

The waggoner's employer, a Major Mundy of nearby Osbaston Hall, was outraged. He sought revenge. The next day he drove the cart himself through the park. Again Sir Wolstan attacked but this time it was he who took the beating.

Years later Sir Wolstan was introduced to King George II as the owner of Bosworth Park.

'Bosworth?' the king said. 'Big battle at Bosworth wasn't it?'

Sir Wolstan replied: 'Yes Sir. But I thrashed him.'

YA BOO SUCKS...

'Multitudinous Frenchmen can pop over rabbits in a furze brake, slaughter pheasants at a battue, shoot hares from behind a rock or a bush, lying *perdu*, at a dead aim; but when we see one Frenchman, born and bred in *la belle France*, do his day's shooting in good style on the moors, throw a fly neatly over a trout stream, or ride even tolerably well across a country, we shall expect to see the next morning a blackamoor washed white, and a leopard change his spots.'

From the Quorndorn Hounds, *by Henry William Herbert, 1856*

✳ Henry William Herbert was America's first professional sports writer. The son of the Dean of Manchester he was born in 1807 and educated at Eton and Cambridge.

Family financial problems forced him to quit England for America in 1831. For eight years he taught Greek and Latin in New York private schools before turning his hand to novel writing. His books were not successful and attracted the criticism of literary giants such as Edgar Allen Poe, who declared unkindly that Herbert was 'woefully turgid' and 'not unapt to fall into pompous grandiloquence'.

Herbert considered taking up law but abandoned the plan after discovering that to be admitted to the American bar he had to become a United States citizen. Herbert was a tremendous snob and liked to boast of his relationship to the Earl of Carnarvon – they were cousins. Becoming a US citizen would have meant him descending to the level of the common man and that would have been unthinkable.

Herbert is best remembered for his sports articles, written under the name of Frank Forester. He spent all his spare time hunting and fishing throughout the north-eastern states and into Canada, and chronicled his adventures in magazine articles and novels. Frank Forester's name became synonymous with field sports.

In private, Herbert was an egotistical drunk with a violent temper. He loved playing the ex-pat aristocrat. A tremendous poseur, he stalked the streets of New York in walrus moustache, checked sport suit, a tweed shawl over his shoulder and jack boots complete with spurs.

He married first Sarah Barker of Bangor, Maine. She died after only nine years of marriage. For the next ten years Herbert took to the bottle and lived alone with only his shooting dogs for company before marrying a woman called Adela Budlong.

Three months after their wedding Adela could stand his drinking no longer and petitioned for divorce. Herbert invited all his literary friends to a dinner party at his rooms in the Stevens Hotel, New York. Only one person turned up. The others sent their excuses.

Herbert and his lone guest had a rather sticky dinner. The guest left soon afterwards. Herbert finished off a bottle of port. Then, standing in front of a full length mirror, he shot himself through the heart.

DWARFS

Possibly the most surreal shooting party yet to take place happened in January 1862 at a blue-rock pigeon shoot on the Hampshire estate of a Member of Parliament called Alexander Baring (rich banker, supremely fine shot and later to become Lord Ashburton) with guests the Bishop of Oxford, the Duke of Argyll and Charles Kingsley, celebrity author of the *Water Babies*.

Having shot all morning, the party broke for lunch. The conversation turned to Kingsley's friend Charles Darwin and his theory on evolution. Darwin's book *On The Origin Of The Species* had been published two years earlier, causing a great stir. Kingsley remarked how the pigeons they had just shot appeared to be different from blue-rocks found elsewhere, notably on the Isle of Wight. He advanced the theory that despite looking different, all pigeons must be descended from one species.

There was muttered agreement from all present except for the Bishop of Oxford, who hated Darwin and everything to do with him. The Bishop dismissed Kingsley's supposition as twaddle.

Now the surreal bit. Apparently determined to outdo Darwin on 'great theories', Kingsley put to the Bishop, the Duke and the MP that there was one big unanswered question: which intermediate species had come between men and apes? Kingsley declared that the only logical answer was elves and dwarfs. He backed this up by claiming that these creatures had subsequently become extinct by natural selection because of competition from the 'superior white race of man.'

Young Baring was reasonably open-minded about this absurd notion. The Duke who had previously described Darwin's writings as 'most curious and original' was, according to Kingsley, 'calm, liberal and ready to hear all reason.'

The Bishop was another matter altogether. Kingsley's proposition that he and his flock were descended from elves must have caused him to blow a gasket.

A few days later Kingsley wrote to Darwin explaining himself: 'It has come home to me with much force, that while we deny the existence of any such intermediate species, the legends of most nations are full of them. Fauns, Satyrs, Inui, Elves, Dwarfs. We call them one minute mythological personages, the next conquered inferior races and ignore the broad fact, that they are always represented as more bestial than man and of violent sexual passion. The mythology of every white race, as far as I know, contains these creatures, and I (who believe that every myth has an original nucleus of truth) think the fact very important. The Inuus of the old Latins is obscure: but his name is from *inire* – sexual violence. The Faun of the Latins…has a monkey face, and hairy hind legs and body – the hind feet are traditionally those of a goat, the goat being the type of lust. The Satyr of the Greeks is completely human, save an ape face & a short tail – The elves, fairies & dwarfs puzzle me, the two first being represented, originally, as of great beauty, the elves dark, and the Fairies fair; and the Dwarfs as cunning magicians, and workers in metal – they may be really conquered aborigines.'

Kingsley added, 'I hope that you will not think me dreaming. To me, it seems strange that we are to deny that any creatures intermediate between man & the ape ever existed, while our forefathers of every race, assure us that they did. As for having no historic evidence of them – how can you have historic evidence in prehistoric times? Our race was strong enough to kill them out while it was yet savage.'

These days such theories would be considered politically incorrect and completely out of order. In those days they caused critics to do little more than choke on their port.

Darwin wrote back saying that Kingsley was quite correct that all pigeons were descended from one species. But he found the dwarf stuff a bit trickier. His friend's 'grand and almost awful question on the genealogy of man' was not a subject into which he wanted to delve too deeply. But he offered: 'If ever intermediate forms…are found, I should expect they would be found in tropical countries, probably islands.'

WHY OLD MEN MAKE FOR BETTER GUNS

'In shooting, experience and the phlegm of age surprisingly make up for the eagerness, alertness and physical fitness of youth.'

From The Wandering Gun, *by John Stanford, 1960*

FROM THE PIGEON TO THE PARTRIDGE

ONE OF THE EARLIEST ANTI-BLOOD SPORT WRITERS was Robert Bloomfield, most successful of the self-taught 'peasant poets' of the Romantic period. Unlike his contemporaries who favoured field sports, Bloomfield, son of an impoverished Suffolk tailor, was strongly against shooting.

Bloomfield's best-remembered work is the epic poem *The Farmer's Boy*, which sold twenty-six thousand copies following its publication in 1800. Here Bloomfield satisfies his hatred of live pigeon trap shooting in a marvellously droll, imaginary letter entitled 'From the Pigeon to the Partridge':

What a long time it is since I received your kind letter about the ripening corn, and the dangers you were presently to be subject to, with all your children. You will think me very idle, or very unfeeling, if I delay answering you any longer; I will therefore tell you some of my own troubles, to convince, you, that I have had causes of delay, which you can have no notion of until I explain them. You must know then, that we are subject to more than the random gun-shot in the field, for we are sometimes taken out of our house a hundred at a time, and put into a large basket to be placed in a meadow, or spare piece of ground suiting the purpose, there to be murdered at leisure. This they call 'shooting from the trap', and is done in this way. We being imprisoned, as I have said, as thick as we can standing the basket, a man is placed by us, to take us out singly, and carry us to a small box, at the distance of fifty or sixty yards; this box has a lid, to which is attached a string, by means of which he, the man (if he is a man), can draw up the lid, and let us fly at a signal given. Every sensible pigeon of course flies for his life, for, ranged on each side, stand from two to four or six men with guns, who fire as the bird gets upon the wing; and the cleverest fellows are those who can kill most; and this they call sport! I have sad cause to know how this sport is conducted, for I have been in the trap myself. Only one man, or perhaps a boy, fired at me as I rose; but I received two wounds, for one shot passed through my crop, but I was astonished to find how soon it got well; the other broke my leg just below the feathers.

O what anguish I suffered for two months, at the end of which time it withered and dropped off. So now instead of running about amongst my red-legged brethren, as a pigeon ought, I am obliged to hop like a sparrow. But only consider what glory this stripling must have acquired, to have actually fired a gun, and broken a pigeon's leg!! Well, we both know, neighbour partridge, what the hawk is. He stands for no law, nor no season, but eats us when he is hungry. He is a perfect gentleman when compared to these 'Lords of the Creation', as I am told they call themselves; and I declare to you upon the honour of a pigeon, that I had much rather be torn to pieces by the hawk than be shut up in a box at a convenient distance to be shot at by a bastard. You partridges are protected during great part of the year by severe laws, but whether such laws are wise, merciful, or just, I cannot determine, but I know that they are strictly kept, and enforced by those who make them. Take care of yourself, for the harvest is almost ripe. I am your faithful 'One-legged friend at the Grange.'

Bloomfield died aged fifty-three in 1823. Having earned a considerable income from *The Farmer's Boy* and subsequent poems, the money was drying up by the time of his death. He left only £40 to be divided among his five children.

TO THE PTARMIGAN

Haunter of the herbless peak,
Habitat 'twixt earth and sky,
Snow white bird of bloodless beak,
Rushing wing, and rapid eye.

Anon, nineteenth century

SIR J'S CORRECT FORM

The most terrifyingly correct gun of the twentieth century was the seed magnate Sir Joseph Nickerson, whose memoirs *A Shooting Man's Creed* went into the bestseller lists upon publication in 1995.

Sir Joseph was a stickler on proper form on the shooting field. Such were his strong views on how to behave he cannot have been an easy guest...

Most shoots in Britain are spoiled by having too many guns. No shoot should have more than seven guns and six is better. Guns should be far enough apart – forty-five yards for normal grouse, partridges and pheasants – and sixty yards for high birds. If you double bank, the front guns should shoot cocks only, leaving the hens for the back row. Drives should be carefully weighted so that each gun fires roughly the same number of cartridges during the day.

Choose your guests carefully. Avoid dangerous and greedy shots. Do not invite guests who do not get on. 'Nothing is worse at a shoot than atmosphere.'

Pheasants and partridges should always be driven. 'Walking up pheasants or partridges and shooting them going away is usually an obscenity.' Walked up grouse however is acceptable 'when properly done.'

Only dense fog or deep snow should lead to cancelling a shoot.

Stops should be placed early in the morning well away from the outside of a wood where the birds can see them when they come down from roost. 'Stopping is a lonely and boring business.'

Laziness should not prevent a keeper from blanking in hedgerows, stubble and coppices first thing in the morning before the shoot begins.

Take a spare gun in case your host suddenly announces it is a double gun day.

Ring your host and cancel at last minute rather than turning up with an infectious cold – especially if other guests are likely to be elderly.

If you do not receive your usual invitation to shoot with Major Snooks, do not be offended. It is probably because in twenty years you have never bothered to ask him back.

Never turn up late at a shoot. Pack your vehicle the night before. Take plenty of cartridges. You will be a nuisance if you run out.

Take enough money to tip the keeper in notes of such value that you will not be asking for change.

Do not arrive at a shoot too early, so you do not fluster the host who has better things to do than entertain you.

It is insulting to the host to turn up with unwashed gum boots or dirty shoes.

Never allow a dog in the back of your vehicle where there are guns in slings on the floor. A heavy labrador can easily break a stock.

Sweepstakes are rather common because they introduce an air of competition.

Guns should be silent going to their pegs and remain silent once on them. 'Nothing alarms birds more than the sound of the human voice or the slam of vehicle doors once the season has started and the birds have begun to realise what it is about.' It is said that some guns attract pheasants over them. 'This is because they remain quiet and are not guffawing and joking on their peg.' The only time beaters should make a lot of noise is when a field of roots or thick cover has to be driven up wind. Otherwise they should tap gently. No shouting! Beaters should come armed only with a stick. No dogs unless a drive is thick with brambles. A well managed shoot should have the undergrowth swiped regularly.

Never shoot low birds except right at the end of the season when too many birds might be left and cause crop damage. Guns should shoot as a team. No bragging about numbers shot. Never shoot a bird which will fly better over your neighbour or further down the line.

Never poach a neighbour's bird. 'To me it is a form of theft, like stealing from somebody's wallet.' (Sir Joseph used to deal with greedy guns by firing off a couple of shots even though there was no bird there. When at the end of the drive the neighbour asked what he was shooting at, he would reply, 'I was just letting you know that I have a gun as well.'

A host should not shout at his keeper in front of his guests if a drive goes badly.

Never move several yards right or left of your peg in order to cash in on birds which belong to neighbouring guns. 'Such people should never be invited.'

Never leave your peg during a drive to pick up a bird. Never go picking up holding a loaded gun because you think you may need to finish off a bird that runs. This happens on the Continent. Never in Britain. Do not let your dog begin to pick up until you have collected the birds close to the peg by hand. Otherwise he will be confused and drop one bird to pick up another. And avoid picking up a neighbour's birds unless you ask permission.

Do not tell anyone how many birds you have shot at the end of a drive unless you are asked. If asked, simply say you had a good stand or a very good stand.

If you are shooting near a cottage and one of your shot birds damages a window or tiles go and apologise immediately after the drive.

Always pick up empty cartridge cases at the end of a drive.

Never tell your host how in your opinion a drive might have been carried out more successfully.

Loaders should not be encouraged to talk unless you want them too. 'Some loaders can be very talkative to an extent which can be boring.'

Hosts should keep smiling even if the day has been a disaster.

Always thank the beaters at a convenient moment during the day.

When you leave at the end of the day make sure you have all your equipment with you. The person who habitually leaves his cartridge bag in someone else's car is a nuisance.

Sir Joseph talks of shoots where the hosts are so greedy that they are determined to draw the best positions. If they have drawn a number which puts them in an unpromising place they are known to suddenly fit in an extra short drive to get themselves two numbers nearer to the action. 'When you see this happening you will know not to go to that shoot again.'

＊ Suprisingly, the well-conected Sir Joseph always shot with an over-and-under, a type of firing piece that is considered rather naff in smarter shooting circles. Indeed, he was the recipient of Purdey's first 12-bore Magnum over-and-under in 1948. In the 1970s he commissioned Purdeys to make him a set of no less than twelve over-and-unders, with thre each of 28, 20, 16 and 12-bores.

THE WOODCOCK CLUB

FLAMBOYANT SPORTSMEN, particularly the type who enjoy wearing club ties, will clamour to gain membership of the Woodcock Club. Entry is achieved by shooting a right and left at woodcock before two witnesses. A right and left means shooting two birds with consecutive shots without lowering the gun between shots. Both birds must be on the wing when you take the first shot. If as usually happens you shoot the first woodcock and the second flushes on hearing the shot, it does not qualify.

Although the club's current sponsors *Shooting Times* like to call the club a 'unique British institution', it was actually started in 1949 by the Dutch Bols liqueur company as the Bols Snippen Club. Members received a bottle of Bols advocat and a tie with a four pin feathers motif.

By 1970 the club boasted more than two thousand members, many of them from Great Britain and Ireland. Indeed, Ireland has always had more than its share of members due to the large numbers of woodcock that migrate there annually. Also, most woodcock shooting in Ireland is walked up meaning that birds are more likely to flush in groups.

The *ST* took over the club in 1983, found sponsorship from J&B whisky and began a tradition of annual black-tie dinners where members could bang on at each other about how they had shot their particular brace. The club does a valuable job in contributing funds towards woodcock conservation.

The current president of the Woodcock Club is the Conservative Member of Parliament and keen shooting man Nicholas Soames. The opportunity to shoot a right and left of woodcock has never presented itself to him, but he says, 'I always hope to have the chance to do so, although I think it is likely that the woodcock would come off better.'

✳ Good stories concerning Nicholas Soames and Prince Philip do the shooting season rounds. Soames was shooting with a nouveau industrialist somewhere in the south of England. At the end of the day the host gathered the Guns and told them that it had been such a good day that they should each give the keeper £100. Soames considered this far too much. He remarked, 'Christ, I only want to tip the man, not fuck him…'

✳ A similar story concerns the Duke of Edinburgh who had just helped shoot around seven hundred head as the guest of a rich chum in Hampshire. Before the Guns went to see the keeper, the host suggested that they should show their pleasure by each tipping the fellow a hefty £60.
'£60,' thundered Philip. 'That's not a tip. That's a wage!'

✳ While on the subject of tipping…it is considered reasonable in 2008 to tip the keeper £10 for the day and then £10 for each hundred birds or part thereof. i.e. a 210 bird day is worth a £40 tip. If it has been a rip-roaring day then you can consider giving an extra tenner.

ENLIVENS THE GLOOM

DURING THE NINETEENTH CENTURY it became fashionable to attach a small bell to the collar of your pointer while shooting woodcock. The idea was that even if you could not see your dog in thick undergrowth you knew it had stopped to point a bird when the bell stopped ringing.

The American sporting writer Elisha Lewis admired this English practice. 'When the covert is very thick it will save the sportsman much halloowing and whistling. The tinkling of the bells, if light and melodious, will not disturb the birds, but rather enliven the gloom and dullness of the woody glens, and add new spirit and life to the sport.'

FLUKE

PRIZE FOR SCOTLAND'S FLUKIEST SHOT goes to a Victorian called Osgood Mackenzie. Osgood, the third son of Sir Francis Mackenzie, laird of Gairloch, in the western Highlands, was stalking near the mouth of the River Ewe when he fired his rifle to see how far away the bullet would hit the water. It was one of those things you do as a young man in an idle moment.

Unfortunately, as Osgood fired three swans were rising from the river. Incredibly, the bullet grazed the tip of one of the swans' wings and down it came.

Young Mackenzie, feeling rather guilty, launched a boat and retrieved the wounded creature. He took it home and put it in a shed with a tub of water filled with barley. For six days the swan nursed its wound (and presumably its injured pride) and refused to eat. Then at the end of the week, the grain was gone.

Mindful that the bird might have difficulty returning to the wild, Mackenzie sent it down by train to London Zoo where it lived for eighteen years. Osgood Mackenzie went on to become a great garden designer. Having bought the Inverewe and Kernsary Estate in 1862 he proceeded to create one of the world's most remarkable gardens. Inverewe Garden, now owned by the National Trust for Scotland, is famous for its exotic species, including Chinese rhododendrons, Tasmanian eucalyptus and New Zealand daisy bushes.

MR CROW

Around 1810 a Mr Crow was elected coroner for Kent, thus prompting the local newspaper to print the following verse:

> One voter to another said,
> The choice, the county now has made,
> For wisdom sure will mark us;
> The world, unanimous, allow,
> No candidate can match a crow,
> To sit upon a carcase.

PICKING UP PIG

STRANGEST RETRIEVER in an English shooting field was a pig belonging to the early nineteenth century baronet Sir Henry Mildmay.

'Slut', as the black New Forest sow was named, belonged to Sir Henry's gamekeeper Mr Toomer. Toomer was training some pointer puppies and the pig, a thin, ugly long-legged creature, would to come along with them.

It occurred to Toomer that a pig could not be more obstinate than the worst dog. And so he would encourage the pig with barleymeal pudding that he kept in one pocket. The other he filled with stones to throw at the pig if she misbehaved. (He was unable to keep her on a lead as he would a pointer.)

Within a couple of weeks Slut got the hang of what it takes to be a gun dog. Very soon she was pointing partridge and rabbits. Eventually she was retrieving as well.

According to a magazine report, 'Her hunting pace was a trot. When she came on the cold scent of game, she slackened her trot, and gradually dropped her ears and tail, till she was certain, and then fell down on her knees. She would frequently remain for more than five minutes on her point. She always pointed straight at the bird, and paid no attention to foot-scent. As soon as the game rose, she returned to Toomer grunting loudly for her pudding.'

Slut became a celebrity. Charles Darwin later wrote her up as a fine example of animal intelligence, (and also presumably as proof of the relationship of man to things porcine.) 'Her scent was exceedingly good and she was more useful than a dog,' Darwin remarked.

GIGANTIC FOLLY

The *London Magazine* of 1827 contained a satirical attack on shooting titled 'The Troubles Of A Game Proprietor'.

> Among those gigantic follies which pervade the great mass of society, and mar its repose and happiness, there is not one, at the present day, more prominent, than the love of sporting in all its diversities,' wrote the anonymous author known only as 'N'.
>
> Of these none is so productive of such serious and extended mischiefs, of so many petty feuds and jealousies, or that can boast of more numerous votaries, than the fashionable mania for the preservation of game, and its destruction by the fowling-piece.

The article included a hilarious imaginary diary as written by a cantankerous landowner in the first week of September...

> SUNDAY – An excellent practical sermon from Dr Rosyphiz on the superlative excellence of charity...Felt a momentary twinge or two when I thought of Hodge. But what if the fellow had been my tenant for twenty years? Did I not freely pardon three different acts of poaching before I turned him out of his farm? And what if he set fire to my haystack and was hanged for arson, and his wife died broken hearted? Was the catastrophe to be referred to my assertion of my just rights of property, or to his own base revenge? As to his six children, they are secure from want in the workhouse. To assert the sacred rights of property is an imperative duty which every man owes to society. On this ground do I strictly resent...the robbery of my game, by peasant or gentleman. Such resentment is no breach of charity. Dr Rosyphix was too general. Why did he not make such an obvious exception? He shan't have his annual brace tomorrow. As to mankind at large, I can survey my feeling towards them with the greatest complacency – with the exception of my immediate neighbours on the right...who are too fond of shooting to allow of our being on the best of terms.

MONDAY – Dreamed I was in the field and came up with a gentleman poacher. Determined not to let the blackguard escape; collared him and shook him. A struggle ensued. Awakened by the piercing shrieks of my wife whom I had nearly throttled with my left hand. The room instantly filled with domestics. A good deal of tittering among the servants – nothing but small beer shall be drank in the kitchen for a month to come. Received a lecture (from wife) on my devotedness to field sports… Sallied out at four o'clock (a.m.) with the major and the rest of my guests. Proceeded to the further extremity of my property on which I had seen several fine covies yesterday. We found not a single head of game, but strong symptoms of their having been netted the preceding night. Returned to breakfast in fuming ill temper. Scalded my throat, broke a cup and saucer, and severely cut my trigger finger. Retook the field…when a succession of shots drew us off to the left. It was clear some rogues were acting in concert. Pounced at length upon three half-pay gentry: a chaplain in the navy, a lieutenant in ditto and an army captain. They refused to give their names and address. Waxed ungovernably wroth, I shot the only sorry quadruped (dog) that all three had between them. This they returned with fearful interest by slaughtering two setters and a high-bred pointer. Moreover the captain and lieutenant saluted me with alternate salvos of naval and military abuse, while the canon of divinity exploded in a formal challenge and talked of a saw-pit as the scene of combat. Compelled to return home in consequence of the loss of dogs. Concocted a furious advertisement for the county paper, offering a reward…adding a minute description of the three banditti.

TUESDAY – Awakened by a loud report near the house, and greeted with the pleasing intelligence that a spring-gun which I had set yesterday had lacerated the leg of one of my keepers in such a manner as to render amputation necessary. Must of course maintain the man for the rest of his life. Ten children! How inconsiderate. Sallied out after an early breakfast. Shot at a bird which fell on my neighbour Tallyho's side of the hedge.

Went after it. Tallyho himself behind the hedge. He taxed me with wilful trespass. Forgot he was a magistrate and swore fiercely. He called on me to pay a fine. Laughed him to scorn. The new dogs, which I had purchased yesterday without a trial on a dog dealer's word of honour turned out to be totally worthless and spoilt my sport so effectually as to send me home at an early hour. On arriving home found a constable carrying off some of my furniture under a distress warrant from Tallyho to raise the fine which I had refused to pay for swearing.

WEDNESDAY – Found the words 'blood-thirsty tyrant' chalked on my walls this morning owing no doubt to my use of spring-guns. Received notice of an action against me by the three half-pay worthies treating my advertisement as libellous.

THURSDAY – Took the coach to A_____ to consult my attorney as to my liability to an action for libel. Found that my three men were but too correct in their law. Met Captain O'Bloodandthunder. He had the impudence on passing his poulterer's shop to ask me to go in with him as he wanted to purchase a hare and a brace of partridges. Out of idle curiosity....I took the liberty of a peep into a back room and beheld in the act of arranging a basketful of game my own gamekeeper, who had obtained permission to go to town that morning under pretence of visiting a dying relation. I had always hitherto considered him the most trustworthy of my menials. He chuckled with delight while he told me that he regularly plundered me, and that all my other keepers had aided in his villainy and shared in the plunder. Returned home in a state of mind bordering on misanthropy. Induced one of my keepers to confess against the rest, whom I immediately had arrested.

FRIDAY – Underwent a terrible trial of temper this morning in an interview with the wives of my imprisoned keepers who brought all their swarms of brats with them. Their tears, backed my wife's, nearly overcame me. But a stern sense of my duty to society, to make examples of these atrocious violators of the sacred rights of property at length brought me through. Took a turn with my gun. In one of my very best preserves found a little monster of five years old taking aim at something or other with a bow and arrow. Took the little prodigy before Rosyphiz. I wished the varlet to be committed to the tread-mill for a month's hard labour. The parson actually refused to commit the culprit at all. Priest and I have shaken hands for the last time. Found to my great indignation that some of the neighbouring villagers had in the course of last night taken advantage of my being without a single keeper and plundered my preserves in the most audacious manner. Not content with that they left a menacing letter at my door threatening to set fire to my house unless I liberated my traitorous keepers.

SATURDAY – Awakened soon after midnight by an alarm of fire. The incendiary writers of the letter had been too faithful to their word by setting fire to several stacks of hay close to my mansion. The flames had communicated to an outhouse. While engaged in extinguishing the flames I had heard several shots fired on my estate. I rushed out with my double barrel. I had scarcely set foot on my lawn e'er a spring gun, which had been removed from a neighbouring plantation by the ruffians who had set fire to my house laid me prostrate the contents severely grazing my thigh. When the catastrophes of the week...passed in mental review, I saw the egregious folly and childishness of such ardent attachment to an idle pastime for the mere sake of selfish amusement. Made a solemn resolution to employ the first hours of renovated health in exterminating every head of game on my estate.

DEAF DOBBIN

IN THE SEVENTEENTH CENTURY gentlemen sometimes took a 'stalking horse' shooting. This was a farm dobbin, preferably elderly and docile, which the shooter walked alongside, keeping out of sight, until rabbit, hare or sitting pheasant was in range. He would then pop round the side of the horse and shoot.

Understandably, the horse had to be extremely long suffering to put up with the gunshot. Not to mention deaf.

In his 1686 book *The Gentleman's Recreation*, sporting writer Richard Blome explains how to train your nag: 'Let your stalking horse be of the largest size, 'tis no matter how old he be, but he must be well trained. Get a strong chain, and fasten it about his head, then tie him up to a tree, and fire your gun near him, giving him your encouragement by voice and hand, stroking him, and so continue shooting near him several times; and although he continue his kicking and capering, yet in about a week's exercise after this manner, he will become so gentle, as to permit you to shoot under his neck, without the least reluctance or stirring. But some are of the opinion, that during this teaching, the horse must be kept waking in the nights, and to shoot under his neck as well as in the day.'

Result: Dobbin has a nervous breakdown. Would have kept the RSPCA busy…

BRIGHT DOG

A TEAM OF EARLY NINETEENTH CENTURY POACHERS working the Earl of Carlisle's Castle Howard estate in Yorkshire dreamed up an original method of taking partridges.

Carlisle's gamekeepers were mystified one night to see a light traversing a field. They prepared to fire at it when the light made a sudden stop and stayed still. They then saw three men come up and surround the light with nets. The keepers pounced…and discovered that the light was a lantern fixed to the head of a setter which had been pointing the partridges. Whenever the dog stopped the poachers knew to draw up the net and capture the birds.

RHINO

I've poached a pickle paitricks when the leaves were turnin' sere,
I've poached a twa-three hares an' grouse, an' mebbe whiles a deer,
But oul, it seems an unco thing, an' jist a wee mysterious,
How any mortal could contrive tae poach a rhinoceros.

G. K. Menzies

(Pickle paitricks = a few partridges; unco = strange)

A BRIEF HISTORY OF THE ENGLISH GAME LAWS

CIRCA 1066. It is a maxim of common law that things to which no one can claim property belong to the Crown by its prerogative. William I introduces the Forest Laws making hunting the sole privilege of the king. He introduces harsh penalties for poaching deer in royal forests: 'Whoever slew hart or hind should be blinded.'

Circa 1080. William Rufus decrees that poaching should either carry the death sentence, or if he is feeling lenient, mutilation including removal of testicles. Nobody is exempt. Nobility and gentry are treated the same as the hoi polloi.

1215. Magna Carta. Laws on poaching in Royal forests relaxed a little. Blinding and de-balling of aristocracy no longer considered acceptable. But it's still death to peasants who dare to poach.

1389. Following the Peasant's Revolt, Richard II rules that the pursuit of game is only lawful if you have good social standing and own land to the freehold value of at least 40 shillings.

Circa 1545. The first game licences in England are granted by Henry VIII. For £20 you can hunt under Royal licence with dogs and bow. But firearms are banned and you are banned from shooting the king's deer or fowl. The poor continue to shoot for the pot illegally even though they risk death by public beheading. There is a thriving blackmarket for guns; for a few quid your blacksmith will knock up some basic barrels and a flint lock.

1603. Sale of pheasants, partridges and hares banned in an attempt to stop widespread poaching.

1671. Law passed allowing a tiny percentage of the population – landowners and lords of the manor of a rank 'not below the degree of Esquire' – to appoint gamekeepers 'who shall have power within the manor to seize guns, nets and engines kept by unqualified persons to destroy game and, by a warrant of the Justice of the Peace, to search in the daytime the houses of unqualified persons upon the ground of suspicion.'

1673. You can now pursue game if you own land worth £100 freehold. Long leases also acceptable.

1723. The notorious Black Act introduced in the wake of a public furore surrounding a group of Hampshire poachers with blackened faces who have been raiding Waltham Chase. The writer Gilbert White reports, 'All this country is wild about deer-stealing.' The new act 'comprehends more felonies than any law that ever was framed before' and provides the death penalty for more than two hundred different offences. The Bishop of Winchester refuses to restock Waltham Chase with deer because 'it has done mischief enough already.'

1770. The Night Poaching Act. For going poaching armed or unarmed between an hour after sunset and an hour before sunrise, a magistrate can give a minimum of three months prison for the first offence, a public whipping plus a minimum six months for the second. But things are looking up. Many landowners ask magistrates to be lenient on poachers. A Victorian commentator remarks, 'Upon the rules of the common law there has been grafted much legislation which up till the end of the eighteenth century was framed for the preservation of deer and game for the recreation and amusement of persons of fortune, and to prevent persons of inferior rank from squandering in the pursuit of game time which their station in life required to be more profitably employed.' Can't put it more simply than that.

1816. New game laws. As shooting gains popularity there is a greater need to protect game. The penalties for poaching become more severe. Even being found in possession of a net at night results in transportation for seven years. The enclosure laws allow landowners to extend their shooting grounds, but deprive villagers of common land upon which to take game. Landowners protect their estates with spring-guns and mantraps. Many gamekeepers are killed as it is in the poacher's better interest to shoot the keeper rather than risk transportation. And you can hardly blame the shilling-per-day labourer for netting the odd rabbit in order to feed his family.

1816. The Bankes Act makes it illegal to buy game. Penalty: £5 per head of game, half going to the informer.

1827. Things are looking up for poachers when spring-guns and mantraps are outlawed by Lord Suffield's bill. (But householders are relieved that you can still set a spring-gun to catch burglars.)

1828. Night Poaching Act introduces transportation for up to fourteen years for poaching in gangs of three or more. Game is defined as pheasant, partridge, black game, red grouse, bustard and hare. (In France game includes everything eatable that runs or flies.)

1831. The slippery slope… The Game Reform Bill makes it lawful for anyone not only landowners to shoot game. Game shooting is now open to anyone who buys a game certificate. Game trading can now be carried on legally if you have a game dealer licence. The fine for day poaching is £5. For night poaching of game and rabbits the maximum penalty on first conviction is imprisonment with hard labour for up to three months. A second conviction means hard labour for up to six months. A third conviction carries a sentence of up to seven years (two years of it hard labour) possibly with transportation. Poachers may be arrested by the owner or occupier of the land or their servants. The 1831 act introduces legal close seasons for pheasants, black game (black grouse), grouse (red grouse and ptarmigan), partridges (grey and red legged).

1844. Poaching penalties are extended to persons found by night on highways in search or pursuit of game. If three or more trespass together on land by night to take game or rabbits, and any of them is armed with firearms, bludgeon or other offensive weapon, they face up to fourteen years penal servitude. 'Night' is from the end of the first hour after sunset to the beginning of the first hour before sunrise.

1862. The Poaching Prevention Act gives rural police the power to search carts and people suspected of possessing poached game. 'Game' now includes the eggs of game birds except, for some reason, bustards. For the first time the police are given direct authority over poachers.

1880. Ground Game Act gives tenant farmers the right to shoot rabbits and hares eating their crops. The courts have established that the right of landowners over wild animals on their land does not amount to ownership so it follows that they cannot prosecute anyone for stealing live wild animals: apart from the game laws, the only remedy against poachers is by civil action.

Nothing much happens to the game laws for another hundred years until…

1981 Wildlife and Countryside Act. Close seasons are introduced for species that are normally considered to be game birds but were not included in the nineteenth century legislation: capercaillie (fully protected in Scotland), snipe, woodcock. Licences cannot be issued under either the Game Acts or the 1981 act to kill or take game birds during the close season. However, in exceptional circumstances, where the birds are causing serious damage, a notice may be issued under Section 98 of the Agriculture Act 1947.

2006. The Game Conservancy describe the present system of game licencing as 'a little daft'. The British Government launches a public 'pre-consultation' on all matters to do with game. They ask questions such as:

Should the requirement to hold both a local authority licence and an excise licence to deal in game be removed?

Should the restriction on dealing in game birds and venison during the close season be removed?

Should game shooting be allowed on Sundays and Christmas Day?

Should the rather ludicrous assortment of game licences be reduced to one? At present there are four types of game licence, each catering for different periods of the year, taking into account the open seasons for various game birds.

Do we still need gamekeepers' licences? A gamekeeper's employer may obtain an annual gamekeepers' licence which at £4 is £2 cheaper than the normal game licence (not exactly a big deal.) (Incidentally, it will cost you £60 for a salmon fishing licence so why not the same for game?) This permits the gamekeeper to take or kill game on land where his employer has the right to game.

Do game seasons need to be adjusted bearing in mind that some aren't even in line with the EU Birds Directive? A note of caution! The Game Conservancy warns, 'While there is always the obvious temptation to encourage Defra to straighten out all the nonsense and bring it into the twenty-first century, there is an even bigger danger that opening up the can of worms will allow too many opportunities to impose a whole raft of further restrictions on shooting and game management.'

2007. The Government announces that it proposes to abolish the need for licences for those who sell and deal in game. In a statement that is surprisingly sensible for a Labour government minister, farming supremo Lord Rooker says, 'We don't need laws that were originally intended to stop peasants killing pheasants. The countryside has moved on a long way since then, and many people in both urban and rural England and Wales would like to sell or eat game. These proposals remove an unnecessary burden from shoots and retailers alike, making it easier for people throughout the country to buy local game.'

HOW TO INSULT YOUR NEIGHBOUR'S DOG

'Ill-bred dogs you may know by their being fox-muzzled, small eyes,
bat-eared, fan-eared, short-necked, head set on like a pickaxe,
broad withers, round shoulders, elbows out, small legs, feet out,
called cat-footed, thick balls*, round barrel, round croup,
clumsy stern, set on low, sickle-hammered.'

From The Sportsman's Directory, *by gamekeeper John Mayer, 1823*

❋ Of feet, not testicles

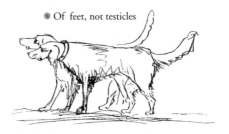

CIVILISED AND CULTIVATED

'In a civilised and cultivated country, wild animals only continue to exist at
all when preserved by sportsmen.'

Theodore Roosevelt, United States President 1901-1909

THIGH OR BREAST

If the partridge had the woodcock's thigh
'Twould be the best bird that ever did fly.
If the woodcock had the partridge's breast
'Twould be the best bird that ever was dress'd.

Anon

HARE WARNING

NEXT TIME YOU SHOOT A HARE, remember that it could be a witch in disguise. Tradition has long been held throughout Europe that witches could change themselves into hares.

In 1662 a woman named Isobel Gowdie, from the highlands of Scotland, was tried on a charge of witchcraft. She told her accusers how she and other witches could transform themselves by repeating: 'I shall go into a hare, With sorrow and sych (such) and meickle (great) care; And I shall go in the Devil's name, Ay while I come home again.' To change back, she would say: 'Hare, hare, God send thee care. I am in a hare's likeness now, But I shall be in a woman's likeness even now.'

Ms Gowdie was evidently quite a one. Other charges included being entertained by the Queen of the Fairies and having sexual intercourse with the Devil whom she described as having an unnaturally cold penis.

Down in Dartmoor there is the legend of the Buckland witch who would send her grandson to direct the local squire's hunt to where he knew a hare would be. The huntsman shot the hare with a silver bullet and then later found the old woman with a bullet wound. The silver bullet was meant to be the only thing that could harm a witch.

Over on the Isle of Man, witches, both male and female, morph into hares so swift that no greyhound, except a black one with a single white hair, can catch them. Meanwhile, in Wales only women from certain families can become hares. In Ireland, it was said that eating a hare was like eating one's own grandmother due to the sacred connection between hares and fairies coupled with the belief that old 'wise women' could change into hares by moonlight.

The Celts used rabbits and hares for divination by studying their tracks and mating dances. It was believed that rabbits burrowed underground in order to better commune with the spirit world, and that they could carry messages from the living to the dead and from humankind to the fairies. Back in Roman times no Celt would dream of eating a hare. And numerous folk tales tell of men led astray by hares who are really witches.

Eostre, the Celtic goddess of fertility (hence the word oestrogen) was said to take the shape of a hare at the full moon. The gestation period of a hare is twenty-eight days – comparable with the moon's monthly cycle. Eostre was often depicted with a hare's head or ears, and with a white hare standing in attendance. This magical white hare laid brightly coloured eggs which were given out to children during spring fertility festivals – a tradition that survives today in the form of the Easter Bunny.

And while on the subject of bunnies...

In Somerset, the appearance of a rabbit in a village street foretells a fire, while in Dorset, a rabbit crossing one's path in the morning is an indication of trouble ahead. Renaissance painters used rabbits to symbolise purity. It was believed that female rabbits could conceive and give birth without contact with a male. Thus virginal white rabbits appear in biblical pictures such as Titian's 1530 painting 'Madonna With Rabbit.'

✳ Legend has it if you dream of a hare you are being warned of an imminent death in the family. If a pregnant woman sees a hare then the baby will be born with a 'hare lip'. It is also said that if a hare crosses the path of a wedding procession then the marriage is doomed.

SAWN-OFF

A STORY IS TOLD AT THE OLD BAILEY of the armed robber who during the 1970s appeared in the dock for holding up a post office.

The police officer who arrested him was in the witness box being cross-examined by defence counsel, a pimply youth with an arrogance generally found in young barristers.

'PC Plod,' said the barrister, 'Am I right in understanding from my client that when you arrested him you called him a cunt?'

'Er, that's right sir.'

The brief pulled himself up to his full five foot nothing. He was on to a winner here. 'And would you like to tell the members of the jury why you used such foul language in front of my client?'

'Well, sir,' said the copper, 'I reckon that anyone who saws off the barrel of a £20,000 Purdey in order to 'old up a sub post office for a 'undred quid 'as got to be a cunt…'

A QUESTION OF LEAD

'To tell a young shooter to aim one foot, two feet or two and a half feet in front of the mark is nonsense; he may as well be directed to aim fifteen to seventeen inches. It is utterly impossible to measure distances in the air in front of a flying bird; instinct alone will teach the hand and eye.'

Quote by Victorian shooting legend Sir Ralph Payne-Gallwey

LIVE PIGEON SHOOTING

The forerunner of the clay pigeon was the live pigeon. Competitive bird shooting became the rage in Regency England. This was the era of Beau Brummel, gambling and decadence. And the swells of the day discovered that there was fun to be had wagering who could shoot the most birds.

Live bird shooting began in London circa 1790 at an Ealing public house called The Old Hatte. As the sport gained popularity, smarter clubs were founded, notably the Hornsey Wood House Pigeon club in 1810. Armed with their best Manton muzzle loaders, gentlemen gathered to blast away at house pigeons while knocking back the best claret and Madeira.

The birds were placed in shallow cavities in the ground and 'trapped' under top hats. A jerk on a line attached to a hat released the pigeon.

Other clubs soon followed including the Red House Club in Battersea, where the annual club cup prize was worth £200 (£10,000 today). And at a famous match at Hornsey in June 1827 two renowned pigeon shots, Lord Kennedy and Squire Osbaldeston, each shot at one hundred pigeons a day for four days for a bet of 2,000 guineas, equivalent to £100,000 today. Kennedy won.

The pigeons at these clubs were netted by farmers in the countryside, often Lincolnshire, and then brought into London and sold to the clubs. Some of the smaller clubs caught up sparrows, starlings and blackbirds in order to reduce costs. However, songbirds were considered inferior targets. Some clubs also employed a practice known as by-shooting where, for a small fee, they allowed the hoi-polloi to gather outside the club grounds and shoot at the birds that had been missed first time round.

The early rules of live pigeon shooting featured a circular ring about one hundred yards diameter. Five boxes, 12 inches long (300mm), 8 inches wide (200mm) and 10 inches (250mm) high, were sunk into the ground five yards apart, parallel to and twenty-one yards from the footmark, from where each gunner in turn would fire. Each box had a sliding lid, which was level with the top of the ground. A designated puller controlled a cord. The shooter would spin a disk numbered up to five. Only the puller, referee and spectators could see what number the disk stopped at. The shooter would give the command to have the box lid released. He was not permitted to put the gun to his shoulder until the pigeon was on the wing. The bird had to fall within one hundred yards of the box or it was deemed a lost shot.

The sport advanced with technology.

As breech loaders replaced muzzle loaders cages replaced tops hats. And because the pigeons were 'trapped' in cages, the pastime became known as 'trap shooting.' Pigeon guns tended to use the tightest choke possible and shooters eschewed safety catches. Live pigeon shots clung on to hammer guns long after game shooters had moved on to hammerless weapons.

The sport caught on in America in 1831 with the founding of a club in Cincinnati. Clubs followed in New York City and Long Island.

Live bird competition shooting was to become the first target of 'antis,' who complained it was cruel. Because of the gambling the sport was considered particularly decadent and in poor taste. Even Colonel Peter Hawker, doyen of early nineteenth century shooting, said that pigeon shooters should 'spare innocent blood' by shooting at pennies instead. Hawker compared live bird shooting to badger baiting. But he added cautiously, 'As it becomes a glorious opportunity for assembling parties to gamble and get drunk, I must not be so unfashionable as to moralise about cruelty; particularly as the professors of this accomplishment might ask me, "Why is it worse than hunting a fox?"'

By 1870 attempts were made to ban the sport in Britain. But it continued at places like London's Hurlingham Club. Hurlingham shoots were grand social events, and the club grew to include polo, tennis, skittles and other upper class pastimes. By the end of the century pigeon competitions were struggling. Few people entered competitions except on the Continent. Big money prizes could still be won in resorts like Monte Carlo.

Ironically, it was Royalty that sought to have the sport banned. Alexandra, Princess of Wales, found the practice so distasteful that she successfully campaigned to have it outlawed, and in 1901 pigeon shooting was abolished at Hurlingham. There is a story that a wounded pigeon flew into Alexandra's lap at a club shoot and bled to death. With such potent opposition as that of the next queen, the sport was doomed. It was banned in Britain in 1906.

✳ The Game and Live Bird Shooting event held at the 1900 Paris Olympics was the only time in Olympic history when animals were killed on purpose. Unfortunately, the event turned out to be quite messy with dead or injured birds all over the stadium. The winners were Leon de Lunden of Belgium (twenty-one birds killed), Maurice Faure of France (twenty birds killed), and Donald MacIntosh of Australia, (eighteen birds killed).

✳ Despite massive public opposition, as of 2007 live pigeon shooting was still legal in a few American states, notably Pennsylvania and Illinois. Attempts at a nationwide ban have been thwarted by the US gun lobby led by the National Rifle Association who say, 'Pigeon shoots are a traditional and international shooting sport. We cannot let this longstanding tradition disappear! Banning pigeon shoots would be a first step in advancing animal rights activists' agenda, and they won't stop there!'

America's most notorious live pigeon shoot of recent years was an annual affair held each Labor Day in Hegins, Pennsylvania. It was shut down in 1999 after the Pennsylvania Supreme Court unanimously ruled that humane officers could prosecute participants for animal cruelty. The judge characterised the event as 'cruel and moronic.' Hegins itself had earned the moniker 'Cruelty Capital of the World.'

✳ Ernest Hemingway loved gambling on live pigeon shooting competitions when he lived in Cuba. Apparently the place to do it was the Club de Cazadores del Cerro in Havana.

SPEED

A NOTED SHOT CALLED COLIN MCLEAN wrote in a letter to *The Field* in 1958 that he had noticed that the one characteristic shared by good shots was speed. 'Their guns came up as their bodies were already moving in the right direction and they pulled the trigger the moment their gunstocks came home to the shoulder – all this in one smooth, coordinated movement of eyes, arms, feet and finger. If one asked them how they did it, they would say that it was merely a question of getting their gun off as soon as it came to their shoulder and never poking.'

INNER SMELL

Little is left to chance when you go hunting in America. The most bizarre shooting accessory to appear on the market is a product called Nullo which is advertised as 'an internal deodorant.' The idea is that you swallow a Nullo tablet and within a short time you start smelling like a polecat. Or rather you cease to emit human smells thus making it easier to get closer to your deer before zapping him with your assault rifle of choice.

Nullo contains the active ingredient chlorophyllin copper complex, designed to control body odours from the inside out. 'It really works,' swear the makers. 'Nullo allows the hunter to get closer to the animals, making for a much more enjoyable and successful hunting experience.' For the hunter, that is.

The makers add, 'No adverse reactions with other medications have been found, however in a small percentage of cases, mild diarrhoea was noted.'

BUNNIES BEHAVING BADLY

The rabbit has a charming face,
Its private life is a disgrace
I really dare not name to you
the awful things that rabbits do.
They have such lost degraded souls
No wonder they inhabit holes.

Anon

KING'S GROUSE

UP IN SCOTLAND A STORY IS TOLD OF KING EDWARD VII who was shooting as a guest of the Earl of Home on his Berwickshire moor. The King had brought with him a Russian count who had never before been in a grouse butt and whose sporting experience had been limited to slotting bears in the woods outside St Petersburg.

For safety, Ivan was placed at the end of the line. The drive began. Pack after pack of black game flew over the Russian's head but he never fired his gun.

Afterwards, the King stomped up in annoyance. 'Why didn't you shoot them?' he demanded.

'Shoot zem?' the count growled. 'But I thought zey were from a chicken farm…'

HOW NOT TO TRAIN

The ten worst practices that will ruin your novice gun dog, according to top American retriever trainer Robert Milner:

Raising your puppy outside in a kennel. 'Any puppy relegated outside to the pen will grow up in relative isolation, deprived of the social interaction that he needs to develop communication skills.'

Making your puppy endlessly retrieve. 'Pup is born with the retrieving instinct. His mother gave it to him. And whether you give him one retrieve or ten thousand retrieves, you are not going to improve his genetic inheritance.'

Repeating commands. 'If Pup doesn't respond to the first command, it's not because he didn't hear you. It's because he doesn't feel like responding. The solution is to trigger the response and reinforce your dominance. You should employ a dominance technique such as a direct, threatening stare or "looming over" body position.'

Shouting at Pup. 'Shouting usually either excites Pup, or makes him afraid. If a 6½ foot NFL linebacker was standing in your back yard yelling at you "You better come over here to me, you blankety blank" would you go to him? Not if you have half a brain.'

Pleading when Pup is out of reach. 'When the dog gets far enough away that we think he's beyond our control, we revert to an asking tone of voice. You know the one. It has a question mark on the end of the vocalisation. If a dog could speak English, you might as well be saying: "Don't obey me. You are beyond my control."'

Letting Pup run off some energy. 'This is a terrible practice. If you regularly let Pup run off energy upon coming out of the house, pen, or car, you are simply training him to be out of control for the first ten minutes around you.'

Giving Pup too many marked retrieves. 'The more marked retrieves Pup gets, the more you are training him to find the bird without help from you. The more you do it, the more difficult it is going to be to convince Pup later that you really know where the bird is.'

Testing instead of training. 'The typical way to teach Pup to do very long marked retrieves is to go out and try it. A helper is sent out one hundred and fifty yards. He gets out there, shoots, and throws a dummy. You send Pup. Pup goes the distance of the longest retrieve he's had. He starts hunting in a circle at thirty yards and never gets out to the dummy. Now you've taught him to fail. Testing Pup to see if he can do what you want is a universal human tendency. It is also universally bad. Always engineer the lesson so that Pup succeeds.'

Experimenting with introductions. Introductions to new things are frequently conducted as an experiment to see how Pup reacts. If you are lucky, Pup will react favourably and the introduction will have been successful. If you are unlucky, the introduction will scare the heck out of Pup and you will have a very big problem that may take weeks to solve. A classic example is to walk up to Pup and shoot off the 12 gauge to see if he's gun shy.'

Changing the rules in the shooting field. 'The two major bad practices you see in the field are (a) never using a leash and (b) sending Pup to retrieve the bird while it's still falling. Many hunters invest hundreds of hours in training their dogs, and then throw away the rules when they get in the field. They forget what a leash is for and let Pup indulge in whatever disobedience he fancies.'

From Retriever Training – A Back to Basics Approach, *by Robert Milner published by Ducks Unlimited (USA), 2005*

THE SNIPE

So swift a bird is apt to make
Young shots with indecision shake;
Such are indebted when they kill
Much more to fortune than to skill.

Anon, nineteenth century

A DESIRABLE INSTINCT

'The instinct for sport is latent in most breasts, and let moralists say what they will, it is in the main a desirable and wholesome one. From how many scrapes – perhaps crimes – has the love of it preserved some of us! A man cannot be doing ill deeds when he is snipe-shooting; he can hardly do much thinking about evil things, unless, perhaps fog tethers him to a hedge side or a peat hag for half a day.'

From Wild Sport And Some Stories, *by Gilfrid Hartley, 1912*

TAKING AIM

Close neither eye – some good shots say,
Shut up your left: that's not my way;
But still a man may take his oath,
He'd better shut one eye than both.

W. Watt, circa 1860

HARE PADDLE

THE HARE IS A GOOD SWIMMER. Hares have been known to cross from island to island off the coast of Scotland. The hare swims with its head shoulders and front paws out of the water and uses all four feet in a kind of doggie paddle or hopping motion. The 1920s shooting journalist Leslie Sprake recalled a hare which regularly swam across the River Test in Hampshire. 'It was the only way it could gain access to a garden in which there was tempting food.'

COURSING - IN MEMORIAM

The tracing hound by nature was designed
Both for the use and pleasure of mankind;
Form'd for the hare, the hare too for the hound,
In enmity each to each other bound.

Anon, nineteenth century

✳ It should be noted that many Victorian sportsmen considered that the hare should never be shot, only coursed. 'They are the indisputable animals of the courser's chase,' is how one writer put it.

FREAK SHOT

SCOTTISH GRANDEE LORD ELPHINSTONE, the sixteenth baron, was shooting grouse in Scotland just before the First World War when a covey of eight birds came towards him. Due to some freak of flight he killed seven with his first barrel. Lord E was so astonished that he failed to fire his second barrel allowing the survivor to pass unscathed.

SPORTING TERMS

To spring or flush partridges

To raise a grouse

To flush or start a woodcock

To spring a snipe or plover

To mark a rail

To start or move a hare

BOND BIRDS

The much celebrated radio-controlled grouse scene in the 1967 James Bond spoof *Casino Royale* was filmed at 12,000-acre Bolton Castle estate on the northern slopes of Wensleydale in Yorkshire.

In the scene, Bond, played by David Niven, was required to pretend to shoot not only the radio-controlled grouse but also the real thing. Which posed a problem since Niven was only an average shot and although he could cope with low pheasants he had little experience of grouse.

The moor's owner Lord Bolton was invited to stand in for Niven so that Bond could be seen to be suitably deadeyed. The peer is credited in the film as 'Lord Bolton – James Bond (grouse shooting scenes.)'.

Bolton who died aged seventy-two in 2001 was a bon vivant who loved hunt balls. In fact, his character was not unlike David Niven's. Bolton was also known for his unruly dogs, not least his infamous spaniel Buster, who once ate a whole goose while sitting in the back of the car during a short journey home from shooting.

AMERICAN RIBALDRY

'AMERICAN WOMEN OFTEN GET KITTED UP at the Scotch House before venturing out into the shooting world, which makes them easy targets for ribaldry especially amongst Scottish keepers. They don't wear scent because they have been told not to, but do wear large gold bracelets clanging with large gold coins because they haven't.'

From Fair Game, A Lady's Guide To Shooting Etiquette, *by Piffa Schroder, Ashford, Buchan and Enright, 1988*

A NEW GUN

THE SPLENDID VICTORIAN shooting 'n fishing writer Augustus Grimble was a jolly bachelor who lived in rented rooms at the Union Club at Brighton.

Most of the time Grimble could be found sponging off friends, either salmon fishing on a Scottish loch or shooting grouse on a moor somewhere. Grimble loved driven grouse but had little time for bad shots. Here he offers the thirty most popular excuses for poor form that could be heard on the nineteenth century grouse moor:

1. Dust in my eyes.
2. Sun in my eyes.
3. Wind in my face.
4. They swerved as I pulled.
5. Could not see them till they were on me.
6. Never saw them till they were past me.
7. The light is so horridly bright.
8. Such a beastly dull light.
9. The butt was too high.
10. A new gun.
11. Had a letter from my wife this morning.
12. So cold I could not swing.
13. Bilious this morning.
14. All the fault of that glass of port after champagne.
15. Fingers so cold that could not feel the triggers.
16. It's drinking that silly lemon squash.
17. A lady in the butt.
18. The loader got in the way.
19. Pipe on the wrong side of my mouth.
20. 'Bacca smoke in my eyes.
21. Too many cigars last night.
22. That whiskey of old Smith's is not good.
23. The cook gave notice this morning.
24. Flo refused me yesterday. (Author's note: it is unclear whether Grimble is referring to a dog, a wife or the shooting box cook.)
25. Boots too tight.
26. Coat cuts my arms.
27. Been threatened with an action for breach of promise.
28. The eggs were hard boiled at breakfast.
29. Birds out of shot.
30. Lost every rubber at bridge last night.

From Shooting And Salmon Fishing, *1892*

FERRET FACTS

Throughout Britain male ferrets are known as 'hobs' except in Norfolk where they are 'jacks'. Females are 'jills' and the young are 'kits'. A castrated male ferret is a 'hobble' and a vasectomised male (yes, really!) is a 'hoblet.'

A group of ferrets is a 'business.'

First historical reference to a ferret is in Leviticus, Ch 11, where the ferret is listed as an animal that Jews must not eat.

Genghis Khan used ferrets for hunting rabbits in the thirteenth century.

First mention of a white ferret appears in Conrad Gesner's 1551 *Historiae Animalum* which describes the white ferret as 'the colour of wool stained with urine.'

Elizabeth I kept a pet ferret.

It is illegal to hunt rabbits with ferrets in the United States. But you can hunt rats with them with a licence.

Most ferrets in America are kept as pets. Much money is spent in pet shops on ferret requisites such as toys and shampoo. Some US states in America are campaigning to ban the public from keeping ferrets as pets because of several nasty incidents involving ferrets attacking children.

The sport of 'ferret legging', which involves placing a ferret down your trousers, originated from the days when poachers hid ferrets in their clothing to avoid detection. It was also a way of warming up your cold ferret after a long winter's day down a rabbit burrow. Until recently it was common practice to stitch your ferret's lips together in order to prevent it biting your bollocks.

The ferret is often used for bio research, particularly into cures for influenza to which the ferret is highly susceptible.

From Complete Guide To Ferrets, by James McKay, *Swan Hill Press, 1995*

SMALLEST SHOOT IN BRITAIN

THE TINIEST FORMAL SHOOT IN BRITAIN is the acclaimed Hauxton Pits near Cambridge where owner Will Garfit manages to produce seven highly respectable drives over no more than sixty-nine acres (twenty-eight hectares) of abandoned gravel pits – ground that is a fifth of the size of London's Hyde Park.

Hauxton Pits is a triumph of conservation. Helped by the Game Conservancy, Will has since 1970 managed to introduce 136 species of bird, twenty species of butterfly as well as a huge variety of game including woodcock, snipe, mallard and geese.

Earth moving equipment was used to transform the land from a sterile quarry into what amounts to a flourishing mini estate. The terrain is a mixture of water, woodland, marsh and arable. The land is bordered by a village high street on one side and industrial wasteland on the other. Hardly ideal conditions for a great shoot.

Will puts down about seven hundred and fifty cock pheasant poults in two release pens. Back in 1980 he tried releasing one hundred partridges but 'they became too tame and were an embarrassment on shooting days running about between the guns.' Wild duck eggs are collected and hatched in an incubator. About one hundred and fifty mallard are released each season, but Will imposes a strict limit on numbers of ducks shot.

Will hosts five shoots before Christmas, with eight guns and a dozen beaters. Early season bags are around one hundred head reducing to thirty-five head later on. There are four or five drives before lunch with everyone walking from drive to drive. 'This is hardly strenuous as during the morning we shoot over only about thirty-five acres,' Will says. The afternoon sees two drives over the lakes. The drives sometimes criss-cross each other but clever tree planting gives the impression that you are shooting over new ground each time.

Will explains, 'It may seem that eight guns is rather a lot for such a small shoot but the layout of the woodland is such that each gun has cover behind him to which pheasants can fly. No one gets a disproportionate amount of the shooting and the bag is made up from each gun perhaps having a chance of a few birds each drive. The guns are stood to make the pheasants most sporting, often in a small glade or amongst tall willows where snap shots test the reaction of even the most accomplished.'

Guests who are used to grander shoots joke about the urbanisation at Hauxton. There are jokes about birds that 'stop' at the traffic lights and Shirley Deterding, one of Britain's finest lady shots, refers to the last drive on the boundary as the Council House Drive since all the guns can see are rooftops above the hedge over which the pheasants are driven.

SIR FRANCIS CHANTREY'S WOODCOCK

NO INCIDENT IN THE HISTORY OF SHOOTING has attracted so much attention as Sir Francis Chantrey's right and left of woodcock – with one shot. This achievement was made even more remarkable by the fact that Sir Francis was blind in his right eye.

Sir Francis was already famous as a portrait sculptor, responsible for the statue of the Duke of Wellington astride his horse at Hyde Park Corner as well as William IV and George IV in Trafalgar Square.

His great woodcock shot happened on 20 November 1829, while he was a guest at Holkham in Norfolk, the estate of Thomas Coke, the noted agriculturalist who was later ennobled as Earl of Leicester. Holkham was Britain's greatest nineteenth century sporting estate rivalled only by Sandringham.

Now you might think that after a week or two of back-slapping and drawing room chit-chat that the excitement of the moment would have quietly subsided.

Absolutely not. Sir Francis, a tremendous self-publicist, ensured that the London newspapers carried endless pieces about his shooting skills. He even carved a marble plaque of the woodcocks and presented it to Coke. This bountiful deed gained Sir Francis yet more column inches in the Press. The plaque still hangs in the Marble Hall at Holkham.

Chantrey lived for another twelve years, dying at the age of sixty. But his legend lived on, nourished by a Scottish writer called James Patrick Muirhead (best remembered as the biographer of steam engine inventor James Watt.)

Muirhead was potty about Chantrey. In 1857 he produced a memorial booklet that can be described as the ultimate shooting fanzine, entirely devoted to the sculptor's triumph at Holkham.

Entitled *Winged Words On Chantrey's Woodcocks*, Muirhead's work must be the longest ever congratulation (or arse-licking) when compared to the brief moment in time it actually took to complete the event.

In no less than 120 pages of poetry and prose, Muirhead goes on and on…and on about that lucky hit.

We learn the precise details: Chantrey was standing in a gravel pit beneath Holkham Hall. His neighbouring gun, a Mr Stanhope, was hidden from him by a bank. Stanhope said at the time, 'Knowing how keen a sportsman he was I was amazed at seeing him running up to me without his gun just at the moment when hares were passing us in all directions. But when I saw him waving his Peruvian hat over his head, and distinguished his joyous countenance, I knew that all was right. "TWO COCKS AT ONE SHOT," burst from him, and he announced to me the feat that he had performed.' Chantrey had shot at one bird exactly the same time as another had got up behind it.

Host Coke was delighted. He declared that the stand should be known in future as Chantrey Hill. He assembled the guns, keepers and beaters and made Chantrey take a salute as he walked passed them. They removed their caps and congratulated Chantrey for 'a memorable fall of woodcocks.' Much was made of the fact that Chantrey was blind in one eye, yet both his eyes, a light grey colour, seemed perfectly healthy.

Even more amazing is that the day before at Holkham Chantrey killed a hare and a rabbit in one shot, though one suspects this was dreamed up later in order to 'big up' the great woodcock triumph. It must also be noted that Mr Stanhope did not actually see the woodcocks being shot but took the sculptor's word for it.

As well as Chantrey, Coke and Stanhope, the other guns that day were a Mr Digby and an archdeacon called Glover, (who was to achieve minor fame for receiving the death bed confession of George IV). The total bag came to 151 head.

Muirhead gushed later in his book: 'No sculptor in Europe had done so much before in the art of shooting.' He then proceeded to launch into an orgasm of verse:

'Go, little book!' and of the sculptor tell
In mingl'd strains of sportsmanship and fancy,
How the two woodcocks, by his dart that fell,
Were rais'd immortal by his necromancy.

As if it couldn't get anymore excruciating than that, Muirhead enlisted the help of Chantrey's friends and acquaintances to assault his readers with yet more dire epigrams.

They ranged from the powerful...

The hand of Chantrey by a single blow
At once laid these united woodcocks low;
But the same hand (its double skill so great)
By single blow their life did recreate.

To the macabre...

Soft as down he carv'd their wings,
Mild as May their faces;
Lovely, loving, languid things,
Fast in Death's embraces!

To the fairly dreadful...

From kindred cocks, when robb'd of life,
How wide the fate we boast!
Their chisel is the carving knife,
Their bed a bed of toast.

To the truly awful...

Chantrey kill'd those woodcocks flying
At a single shot;
They, as life departed, sighing
'Now we go to pot!'

To the tragic...

Rais'd to the sylvan genius of the place,
Stands this fair marble, blest by every grace:
Where feather'd forms, warm-breathing, softly tell
How by one fate two hapless lovers fell.

To the hearty...

He shot them, and ate them, and sculptur'd them too;
I wish, my dear Chantrey, that I had been you!
In art, sport, or feasting, let Chantrey alone
For cleverly killing two birds with one stone!

To the inaccurate...

Each bullet, they say, has its own proper billet,
And sharp must a shot at a cock be, to kill it;
But here is a trigger, when neat fingers pull it,
That brings down two bills and two cocks with one bullet!

To the political…

A rare success was Chantrey's lot –
He bagg'd us at a single shot;
And, to commemorate his skill,
In marble made this Re-form'd Bill!

To the classical…

Uno conatu felix, unaque sagitta,
Chantreii binas dextra cecidit aves;
'Arte mea cecidistis,' ait; 'potiora repono,
'Arte mea aternum vivite marmoreae.'

Not everybody was convinced. The gossips doubted whether Sir Francis had actually shot the birds. After all, nobody actually saw him do it. And one anonymous bard was quite cheeky:

'Luckless our fate – a double luckless lot!
A sportsman carved us whom an artist shot.'

✳ More Chantrey woodcock trivia. Fellow artist Sir Edwin Landseer included the two woodcock in a painting of Chantrey's Dandie Dinmont called Mustard, which had been given to him by the novelist Sir Walter Scott. The picture showed Mustard intently watching a cat, which in turn has its eye on the woodcock.

✳ Some remarkably flukey shots were reported during the mid-nineteenth century and one has to wonder whether the celebrity achieved by Chantrey encouraged others.
   In 1856 a Lieutenant Kirkes R.N. claimed he brought down six snipe out of a wisp of seven. His son, Captain Kirkes, went one better when he used a single barrel to kill a grouse on the wing and two hares sitting. Later that year a man called Croft killed no less than 118 plovers in one shot from a punt gun loaded with a pound of lead.
   It was no different abroad. A Dr Sandwith who was shooting on a branch of the Euphrates near Erzeroom, Armenia, bagged four spoonbills in one shot. Even Chantrey's number one fan, Muirhead himself, claimed to have killed two partridges with one shot.

FROM GROUSE TO ICE

EDWARD WILSON (1872 to 1912) is best remembered as the scientist who died with Captain Scott on the ill-fated Antarctic expedition.

What is less known about Wilson is that he was once Britain's greatest authority on grouse. From 1905 to 1910 he was the chief field observer to the Grouse Disease Commission which was established to discover the origins of the illness that was decimating Britain's grouse population.

Educated at Cheltenham and Cambridge, Wilson was a self-taught artist and field naturalist. In his early twenties he contracted tuberculosis from his mission work in the London slums, but recovered enough to be appointed zoologist on Scott's first expedition aboard *Discovery* in 1901.

When Wilson first took on the grouse disease job he expected it to last six months. But soon dead grouse were 'pouring in by every post' to the family home in Hertfordshire. Every dead grouse found on a British moor was dispatched to Wilson and during the course of the enquiry he would dissect nearly two thousand birds. One of Wilson's colleagues remarked that Wilson was constantly surrounded 'by a halo of grouse feathers and unraveled entrails which were popular neither at home, nor in the hotels he stayed in as he travelled around the country.'

However, there was an irony to Wilson's work. Despite having done a considerable amount of shooting in his youth, Wilson was by now anti-blood sports. But he wisely kept his views to himself for fear of upsetting the countless landowners and gamekeepers who were sending him dead grouse. Indeed, he gained great respect from keepers who realised that Wilson understood much more about the habits, biology and predators of the grouse than they did. Wilson's research led him to discover that the disease was being caused by a threadworm in bracken.

In 1907 Wilson received an unexpected invitation from Ernest Shackleton, who asked him to be second in command on his expedition to the South Pole. Wilson declined because of his grouse work.

Two years later Wilson received the call from Scott. Wilson decided he had had enough of grouse and wanted to return to serious exploration. In June 1910 he sailed south with Scott on *Terra Nova* as chief scientific officer.

The final report of the Grouse Disease Commission was to establish Wilson as one of the great ornithological pioneers of the twentieth century. But he would never see the results of his work. Having been beaten to the Pole by Roald Amundsen, Scott's team faced a difficult return journey to their base camp. Overcome by the weather, Wilson died, along with Scott and the three other team members, in February and March 1912.

Wilson had been Scott's closest comrade on the expedition. Their bodies were found eight months later frozen in their sleeping bags, Scott's left arm around Wilson.

ENCOURAGING WORDS

ENCOURAGING WORDS FOR THE NOVICE SHOT from 1920s shooting expert Robert Churchill: 'Keen eyesight in shotgun shooting is comparatively unimportant. A man who can't hit a golf ball or pot a black to save his life can shoot driven game with fair precision provided only that he can see well enough to distinguish a flying pheasant from a partridge at about thirty yards…'

DON'T TELL PLOD...

'Different keepers have different ways of dealing with poachers, but the best keeper is he who will prevent poaching by some other means than having the delinquents up before the magistrates. I knew of one, who, when he had good evidence that a man had been poaching, went and picked a quarrel with him about some trivial matter and gave him a good thrashing. The culprit knew well enough what the punishment was for, and poaching on that shoot was, after a short time, practically unknown. It is not given to every man, however, to be able to beat his fellows, so this plan of stopping poaching is not likely to become general, but having the delinquent up before the Bench should be the last resort. It is very disheartening, if, on catching a man red-handed, and knowing that he had a lot of game off your shoot, the Bench fines him five shillings which he pays at once and goes off laughing.'

Sound advice from Shooting On A Small Income,
by Charles Walker, 1900

IGNORANT ANTIS

IN 2003 the animal rights group Animal Aid sent a pack of 'joke' playing cards to Princes William and Harry featuring amateurish cartoons of Royal Family members out shooting. The number 5 card depicted beaters throwing some newly released birds up into the sky with the ponderous caption: 'Reluctant to fly into the line of fire.' Which sums up how much the antis understand shooting...

FOUR TONS OF SHOT

The first Englishman to keep a detailed game book was James, second Earl of Malmesbury (1778 to 1841). Highly entertaining it was too.

During a lifetime of sport Malmesbury recorded a total of 54,987 shots for 38,934 head of game, in pursuit of which he had walked 36,200 miles or 'very nearly once and a half the circumference of the Globe.' He reckoned that he had fired about four tons of shot and 750lb powder, and had never suffered a day's sickness.

An early entry, on 17 October 1799, detailed an invitation from Prince Esterhazy (patron of the composer Haydn) to a pheasant and hare *chasse* at his hunting estate at Hinkenbrunn, Hungary.

Malmesbury recalled that eighteen guns assembled for coffee at 11am before setting off for the 'field of battle' – a wood surrounded by a net about four feet high guarded by women and children at hundred yard intervals. The whole of the preceding day and night huge numbers of peasants had driven game into this netted area.

'The first measure was to allot to every shooter his post. Eighteen stakes were numbered for that purpose, a ticket corresponding with that number having been previously given to us, and we had each of us the path pointed out that we were to pursue. Each man was at about twenty yards from his neighbour, and this intermediate space was filled up with peasants, so that the whole formed a complete and almost compact line... Each shooter had three people to attend him for the purpose of loading his guns, of which he had a relay of six, carried on a stand behind by a peasant. Some of us had for loaders grenadiers from the Prince's body-guards, the finest men I ever saw.'

Malmesbury described how lines of guns and beaters walked through the wood flushing pheasants in bunches of fifty at a time. Then the party turned round and did the whole wood again. The process was repeated six times. Nothing escaped the guns.

The bag was 1,008 head – 211 hares, 788 pheasants, six partridges and three woodcock. Lord M's share came to 109 head. He shot with seven guns, mostly borrowed.

'For novelty and magnificence the day was one of the finest sights I ever beheld,' Malmesbury declared, 'Though in point of sport it was little inferior to a butchery...'

THE PLOVER

The tireless notes from cuckoos' throats
Proclaim the advent of the spring;
The nightingales' melodious wails
their vernal message bring;
From myriad beaks come cheerful squeaks,
On cocoa-nuts where coal-tits cling,
While tuneful trills from blackbirds' bills
Make all the meadows ring.
Yet where can any man discover
A bird more pleasing than the plover.

On velvet lawn, from early dawn,
The stately peacock loves to fling
His fan of eyes towards the skies,
And shrieks like anything;
Jackdaws and jays their voices raise,
Wild geese make music on the wing,
And all day long their jocund song
The larks at Heaven's gate sing.
But though they scream or soar above her,
No feathered fowls can match the plover.

The Devout Plover, by Harry Graham, *1909*

✳ Incidentally, although it has absolutely nothing to do with shooting, Graham's best known verse
is too good not to be reprinted here:

Billy, in one of his nice new sashes,
Fell in the fire and was burnt to ashes;
Now, although the room grows chilly,
I haven't the heart to poke poor Billy.

POLICE PRIORITIES

I N OCTOBER 2006 NO LESS THAN EIGHTY POLICE, complete with helicopter support, descended on houses near Leadhills in Lancashire following complaints that game keepers had been poisoning birds of prey such as golden eagles and red kites.

Similar dawn raids in Angus, Scotland, involved twenty-five police officers, backed up by assorted civil servants from various government agencies.

Women and children were woken and generally harassed. Keepers were taken away for questioning. All were later released.

No charges were brought.

Point of this story: the next time you are burgled or mugged, particularly in Lancashire or Angus, ask the police why they could not provide you with half a dozen panda cars and a helicopter in order to catch the culprits.

Meanwhile, the National Gamekeepers' Organisation issues guidelines on what to do in the event of a police search. Here is an abridged list of their suggestions:

1. Stay calm! Police must have a warrant to search premises and if they are accompanied by civilians such as RSPB or RSPCA inspectors, you should point out to the police officer in charge that the warrant only authorises the police to search and not those accompanying them. A RSPB man for example can examine birds' eggs but not search for them.

2. If the warrant specifies a search for certain things the search cannot continue once those things have been found. The officers cannot go 'fishing'.

3. Searches must be conducted with consideration for property and the privacy of the occupier of the premises. But force may be used if the occupier refuses to cooperate.

4. If cautioned make it clear you will not say anything without your solicitor being present. Do not be drawn into apparently innocent conversations about your job.

5. N.B. Keep your gun licences in order and available. Likewise abide by the rules of storage of firearms, ammunition and vetinerary medicines.

6. Build 'bridges' with the local police so that you are known and respected by them. (i.e. if possible, take out Plod for a drink from time to time.)

7. After a raid make written notes immediately while events are fresh in your mind.

8. Report the raid to your NGO regional chairman and if you have a complaint write to the Chief Constable.

10. Do not get into arguments with the police.

JOSEPH MANTON

The man responsible for the modern London gun trade was Joseph Manton, of whom one of his craftsmen, a certain James Purdey, said, 'But for Joe we should all have been a parcel of blacksmiths.' Manton, born 1760, became Regency England's most celebrated gunsmith. By 1820 every serious shooting gentleman in the country boasted a Manton. They were finely balanced guns, beautifully engraved and more accurate than anything that had come before.

Joseph began his gunmaking revolution as apprentice to his older brother John, himself a successful gunsmith in London's Dover Street. Although it is Joseph who has gone down in the history books as the great gunmaker, he could not have done it without John's guidance.

Young Joe opened his solo venture in 1792 in Davies Street, off Berkeley Square, London. The shop was an instant success. Shooting men learned that Manton guns performed better than anyone else's. Business boomed and Manton boasted, 'I shall continue annually to increase my charges by five guineas, and still no gentleman will be without a Joe Manton.'

Until then the double barrelled shotgun was a novelty trusted by few serious sportsman. Manton revolutionised sport shooting by introducing an elevated rib which rested above the two barrels thus giving greater accuracy. Few guns up to then had been rifled. Manton invented a mechanism that made it easier to rifle a barrel. He also refined shot design to make for faster reloading and gave his guns lower front sights so that people would shoot above where they thought they were, thus preventing underneath shots, a common novice error with muzzle loaders.

Manton's obsession for perfection was his downfall. As well as making sporting guns, Manton was working on a new type of ammunition for the British Army's artillery. Around the time of Waterloo he had invented a system whereby a cannonball could be connected to a sack of gunpowder, thereby eliminating the need for powder and shot to be loaded separately. This was the forerunner of the modern artillery shell and paved the way for breech loading weapons, thus giving Manton the dubious accolade as the father of the means for modern warfare.

The project fell apart due to a row over money. Manton believed the Army owed him £30,000 for his design. But the Government argued that they had already invested a large amount in research and did not want to give away such a huge sum for a design that had not been properly tested. Manton retaliated by patenting his design in order to force the Army to strike a deal. The Army made a counter offer of one farthing for each shell produced.

Manton turned them down, expecting them to up their price. The Army told him to get lost. And that was the end of their relationship with tricky Joseph. Years of legal battles followed, during which Manton lost his fortune. He was declared bankrupt in 1826. His stock of guns was taken over by his former employee Joseph Lang, who went on to form Atkin, Grant and Lang.

Manton ended up in prison for debt. He was released but his spirit was broken. He died in poverty in 1835. His old friend Colonel Peter Hawker, legendary game shot, paid the funeral expenses.

Hawker had spent much time with Manton helping him to perfect the sporting gun. He wrote the inscription on his friend's tomb: 'To the memory of Joseph Manton, who died, universally regretted, on the 29th day of June 1835, aged 69. This humble tablet is placed here by his afflicted family, merely to mark where are deposited his mortal remains. But one everlasting monument to his unrivalled genius is already established in every quarter of the globe, by his celebrity as the greatest artist in firearms that ever the world produced; as the founder and father of the modern gun trade, and as a most scientific inventor in other departments, not only for the benefit of his friends and the sporting world, but for the good of his king and country.'

In private, Hawker was more outspoken. He wrote to a friend, 'From wealth, Joe was reduced to want, by the assistance of lawyers and the patent laws.'

The Manton legacy lives on with the names of his remarkable craftsmen...

James Purdey set up business on his own in Manton's former Oxford Street premises, later the site of D H Evans department store. (Manton and Purdey were connected outside office hours by the fact that Manton had married Purdey's daughter.)

Charles Lancaster, Manton's barrel borer, and William Greener, who set up shop in Birmingham, both became famous gunmakers in their own right. Greener's greatest achievement was inventing a half-inch bore whaling gun that could throw a harpoon forty yards. Thomas Boss, another Manton craftsman established his own London business in 1830.

✳ Manton also revolutionised the duelling pistol. He noticed that the recoil from most pistols of the day tended to force back the shooter's forearm, causing the gun to jerk upwards as it was fired. Manton produced a pistol with increased the weight at the front end of the barrel thus steadying the gun.

✳ Some Americans have been fooled into thinking that they own a rare Manton. Circa 1900 a Belgian company calling itself J. Manton and Co. was exporting container loads of low grade shotguns to America. It was an invented name and had nothing to do with real Mantons.

✳ Gun geeks will know that the early nineteenth century Manton dispelled no more than one hundred and ten pellets to the thirty-inch circle, compared to more than two hundred pellets of the modern shotgun.

NON PC

Gratifyingly non-PC advice from the 1816 manual *The Shooter's Guide*: 'As a means of attaining the art of shooting flying, young sportsmen are advised, by the injudicious, to shoot at swallows; and many, I doubt not, after succeeding with some of these birds, have been chagrined beyond measure to find themselves wholly unable to bring down a partridge. The practice, I am persuaded, is of little or no service; the flight of a swallow being so very unlike that of any bird which is the object of sport. However, shooting at sparrows will be found a better practice, and perhaps the best, from their flight resembling that of the partridge. An indifferent marksman, I have no doubt, may derive benefit from it.'

BIGGEST VERMIN HUNT IN HISTORY

THE BIGGEST VERMIN HUNT IN HISTORY took place in North America during a week in April 1856 at the village of Frost, in the county of Shefford County, Quebec, Canada. The residents assembled at the Golden Eagle Tavern to discuss how best to rid themselves of the vast amounts of wild creatures devastating crops and forests.

One hundred and fifty armed men set off into the countryside. The nineteenth century American shooting commentator Benedict Revoil reported, 'It was resolved that the marauding birds and quadrupeds should be made the subject of a kind of massacre of St. Bartholomew.' By the end of the week the bag amounted to an incredible 82,804 head, including 74,770 red squirrels, 4,430 jays, 1,140 woodpeckers and 300 owls. But it is worth noting that they shot only one pigeon.

Revoil noted, 'Sport is so abundant in North America that the sportsman more frequently finds his ammunition run short than any lack of game.'

DEFINITION OF A ROUGH SHOOT

'A ROUGH SHOOT MAY BE A MARSH, A HEATH, A MOOR; it may or may not have a wood, it may be literally rough or not rough at all; it may in fact consist of any type of land imaginable. But the distinction of a rough shoot is that it has no fully qualified or recognised keeper and that no large-scale rearing of birds is done within its grounds. The keeper and the rearing-field go together – they are indispensable to each other. When a rough shoot has either of them (unless the tenant is his own keeper) it ceases to be a rough shoot and climbs higher up the social scale. The true rough shoot is what its names implies, a happy-go-lucky, hope-for-the-best piece of land. Size alters its status not one whit. Of course, if there is a wood on the land, pheasants may be reared; but not to the extent of three thousand birds tendered by two professional keepers.'

From Rough Shooting, *by Julian Tennyson, 1938*

A PROPER DINNER

Mince a woodcock. Add an ounce of breadcrumbs to the mince. Moisten with a little brandy or cream and include a little shredded suet. Insert stuffing into a pheasant and roast.

Recipe from The Field

BALLS

Before the clay pigeon came the glass ball. The balls were two and three quarter inches in diameter, about the size of a cricket ball. They were often stuffed with chicken feathers so that when smashed the feathers came fluttering down resembling a shot bird. Sometimes they were filled with talcum powder thus producing a 'puff of smoke' when hit.

Glass ball shooting originated in Boston, America in 1866 as a result of the revulsion felt by many for using live pigeons in shooting competitions. The first competitive target shoots were organised by a Bostonian called Charles Portlock. However, the game did not have great success at first because the rudimentary traps could only throw the balls a short distance into the air making them easy to hit. This was not much of a challenge to a shooter who was used to a fast flying pigeon which could tear off in any direction.

A decade later an American professional shot called Adam Bogardus patented a trap which could hurl balls at least sixty feet through the air in a long arc. Bogardus also patented various designs of glass target balls, including a raised diamond pattern on the surface of the ball which prevented shot from ricocheting.

Rules were drawn up for this type of shooting. The shooter was to be eighteen yards back from the traps and the balls had to fly at least sixty feet in the air. A game would use three traps hidden from the shooter's view. The left trap threw the ball to the left, the centre trap hurtled the ball straight ahead and the right trap threw the ball to the right. The shooter never knew which type of shot he would get. The challenge was to shoot one hundred balls in the shortest period of time.

The early glass balls, which were blown in molds at the end of a blowpipe and cost a dollar per hundred, were much harder to break than today's clay pigeons. Also, ball shooting was a health and safety nightmare. Glass fragments could blind you. You did not want to be looking upwards when a ball was shot.

Bogardus held about every shooting record going, including the extraordinary achievement of breaking the most targets in one day – 4,844 out of 5,000 in 500 minutes. One can only imagine the state of his ears. As well as being an outstanding shot, Bogardus was an insufferable egotist who described himself in his biography as 'Champion Living Shot of the World.'

The other great glass ball shooter was a commercial buffalo hunter from Illinois called Doc Carver. In 1877 Carver published a challenge to 'any man in the world' to shoot at five hundred glass balls from twenty-five yards for five hundred dollars. He hoped to attract a match with Bogardus. But Bogardus played hard to get, terrified he would be beaten.

For the next six years Carver travelled America and Europe giving shooting exhibitions. He became more famous than Bogardus. Eventually, Bogardus could stand it no longer and agreed to meet Carver at a match in Louisville, Kentucky, in 1833. Carver won by one ball.

Bogardus challenged him to a best of three. The second and third matches were held in St Louis and Chicago, this time using new-fangled clay targets, or 'clay pigeons.' Again, Carver won both times. Bogardus was humiliated. His bravado had gone and he was forced to admit publicly that Carver was the better shot.

✳ A few glass target balls have survived in America...but these days they are used as Christmas tree ornaments.

THE BEATER

AMERICAN SHOOTING AUTHOR Peter Blakeley attempts to explain to his readers the role of a beater on an English country estate: '...On all driven shoots the birds are pushed out over the waiting guns by beaters. They are local guys who do it for the love of the game. They usually happen to be (self professed) experts on such interesting topics as fishing, fighting, ferreting, the consumption of alcoholic beverages, and the anatomy of pretty ladies. They are the backbone of the shoot. The success of the drive and the hard work of the gamekeeper ultimately depend on a good supply of knowledgeable beaters. They line out in a regimented fashion, perhaps thirty yards apart, at the edge of the woods, and then tap their way through with hazel sticks, braving the tangle of undergrowth, inclement weather, hangovers, unruly livestock, and low shooting guns, all to flush the birds...'

WILLIAM WATTS

THE INVENTION of mass-produced lead shot by a Bristol plumber called William Watts was the result of a drunken nightmare.

The story goes that having gone to bed after a heavy evening on the sherbert in 1782 Watts had a near-hallucinogenic dream where he saw his wife standing on a local church tower pouring molten lead on him through the holes in a rusty frying pan.

Until now shot had been of random size and full of imperfections. Following his dream, Watts experimented with the height of the drop and devised the idea of the shot tower. He took out a patent for his process describing it as 'a method of making small shot solid throughout, perfectly globular in form, and without the dimples, scratches and imperfections which other shot, heretofore manufactured, usually have on their surface.'

Watts turned his Bristol house into a shot factory. He cut a hole in the floors and dug into the basement. On the roof he put a tower giving a total drop of ninety feet. Molten lead was poured through a pan with calibrated holes. As it fell, surface tension formed the droplets into spheres. Cooled thoroughly when it hit the water below, the rough shot was dried, sorted and polished. All went well until the basement flooded when the River Avon was at full tide and Watts's neighbours complained about the smell.

In 1787, Watts built a shot tower in London and made enough money to go into building speculation. This proved to be a disaster. He went bankrupt during the slump caused by the Napoleonic Wars.

✳ Watts was immortalised in an excruciating poem by Bristol bard John Dix:

'Mr Watts very soon a patent got
So that very soon only himself could make Patent Shot;
And King George and his son declar'd that they'd not
Shoot with anything else – and they ordered a lot.'

ESSENTIAL TIPS FOR GUNS

Hints courtesy of 'Marksman' writing in the 1860 shooting book *The Dead Shot*:

❧ Do not toil too hard at shooting, particularly if you are not very strong. Over-exertion weakens the nerves and injures the constitution.

❧ The sportsman, during the month of September, should never take the field without a knife, a drinking horn, and a shilling for largesse.

❧ By keeping a few of the most central fields on your manor quiet, and seldom shooting in them, you have always a nursery to which your frightened birds will resort.

❧ Always allow game to cool thoroughly before packing it or you may have the mortification of receiving an acknowledgment from your friends at a distance, of a hamper of game, which arrived 'un peu trop haut.'

❧ Never press the trigger unless certain that your aim is true; and never vary your eye from the bird you first fix upon as the object of your aim.

❧ When a sportsman misses several shots in succession with one barrel...he should use the other exclusively for some time.

❧ The young sportsman must always shun spirits; the old one sometimes requires a stimulus of the kind to help him over the hedges, and to lift his legs out of the heavy soil fallows.

❧ In shooting with a young sportsman, or a stranger, always allow him to precede you in getting over the fences; it may be that you save your life by the precaution. (Because he may shoot you with his cocked muzzle loader.)

❧ Always correct and point out errors which you observe in young sportsmen, and rebuke anyone, whether old or young, in whom you detect carelessness in handling the gun.

❧ If being no sportsman yourself, you invite one or two friends to shoot over your manor, do not offer or propose to 'walk with them'. Sportsmen always enjoy the sport more if unaccompanied by the non sporting friend who invites them. But do not forget to send them a luncheon. Very hard toil sometimes belongs to shooting and sportsmen, generally, have keen appetites.

❧ However generously disposed you may be towards your friends and neighbours, if you have a valuable dog, never lend it. And the same may be said of a favourite gun.

PARTRIDGES IN IRAQ

Thanks to the American and British occupation of Iraq, the partridge has made an unexpected comeback in the country. But there's no chance of a good driven day in Iraq just yet.

The Black Francolin, known locally as the black partridge, was shot almost into extinction during the Saddam years. But these days it is out of the question for any Iraqi to carry a gun – whether it be a Purdey or an AK47. Which has meant the bird's revival, particularly on the southwestern outskirts of Baghdad.

Local farmers say partridges are now commonplace. One smallholder complained his farm was being overrun by them. 'I wouldn't mind shooting them but if I do the Americans will probably shoot me,' he said. 'The birds come right up to my door. It's as if they know they are untouchable.'

Hunting was a favourite pastime in pre-war Iraq. Saddam Hussein and his sons were known to be keen shots. Alas, the best Iraqi shoots, south of Baghdad, along the banks of the Tigris and Euphrates, have since become terrorist strongholds.

FIRST PHEASANT FANCIER

THE FIRST PERSON TO MENTION THE PHEASANT as a domestic fowl was the fourth century Roman writer Rutilius Taurus Aemilianus Palladius.

Palladius gives directions for the care of pheasant eggs and chicks: '…Only young birds should be used for breeding, that is birds of the preceding year. Pheasants mate in March or April. One cock will do for two hens, for the pheasant is not such a tyrant in love as are some other breeds. The hen has one brood in a year, about twenty eggs. It is best to incubate these under ordinary barndoor fowls and each foster mother should cover fifteen eggs. The young birds hatch on the thirtieth day. For the first fifteen days they should be fed on barley meal steamed and cooled off and on the meal a little wine should be sprinkled. Later you should give them kibbled wheat, locusts and ants' eggs.'

Apart from the small matter of finding locusts in England (though anything is possible with global warming), the methods of feeding are more or less the same as they are today.

HOLLAND AND HOLLAND

UNLIKE his gunsmith contemporaries, Harris Holland, born 1806, founder of Holland and Holland, began his career as far removed from guns as you can get. In the 1830s he was running a wholesale tobacco business in Holborn, London.

Holland's great love was shooting. He was a good shot and was a member of two fashionable London pigeon shooting clubs, the Old Red House and Hornsey Wood. He was also well off enough to lease a grouse moor in Yorkshire.

Tiring of tobacco, Holland turned his hobby into a lucrative business. He developed a sideline

dealing in guns and friends convinced him to start his own gun business. His first shotguns, produced in the 1840s, were built in the trade to his design. A decade later he was making his own, each bearing the inscription H. Holland.

Harris was unusual when compared with the likes of Purdey, Boss and Lang, who had come into the gun trade as young apprentices. Also, Harris had no connection with gunmaker Joseph Manton who had spawned most of the London gun trade.

Harris had no children of his own. In 1857 at the age of fifty-two he took on his nephew Henry as an apprentice. Ten years later Henry became a partner. And so was born the famous name of Holland and Holland. But Uncle Harris still held a tight reign and only he was allowed to sign cheques. By the time of Harris's death in 1896, the firm owned a large factory off London's Harrow Road making shotguns and rifles. H and H's present factory lies only a few hundred yards away.

✱ Holland & Holland trivia. During World War I the firm was commissioned by the Admiralty to produce a special anti-Zeppelin shotgun. This spectacular weapon fired a form of chain shot through a choked barrel that would rip through the fabric of a German blimp. About 130 were issued to the Royal Naval Air Service.

DEGRADED FRENCHMEN

THE VICTORIANS had a hatred of French partridges. Many keepers regarded them as little better than vermin and did everything they could to destroy them.

The shooting writer 'Marksman' told readers of his 1860 book *The Dead Shot* that they should destroy French partridge nests in the spring and 'kill the old birds during deep snows when they are unable to run but hide in the hedge rows and neighboring woods.'

It was thought that French partridges did not fly as well as their English cousins. The problem was that upon seeing a dog or a gun, the Frenchman would run before rising a long way off, out of range of a

muzzle loader. Worse. When he was cooked he didn't taste as good as an English partridge.

The French partridge's refusal to fly properly would ruin a gun dog, claimed Marksman. 'They spoil the dog, make him unsteady, over anxious and doubtful. French birds are always reluctant to fly until they have run a long distance, sometimes cross two or three fields and it is only by a thorough knowledge of their habits, and by cunning and perseverance, that a sportsman can get a shot at them.' Marksman concludes with a flourish. 'The sportsman should keep down the race of the French!'

Similar views were held by William Carnegie, author of the 1883 *Practical Game Preserving*, which contains the first detailed instructions for shoot management. 'The red-leg, except during downright cold weather, or the first week in September, is almost "ungetatable",' Carnegie fumed. 'Gastronomically speaking, they are worth no more than a pigeon, while the way in which they thrive themselves and steadfastly endeavour to preclude their less gaudy brethren from doing so, is no qualification for them as a British game bird. Under these circumstances, the best thing to be done is to clear them off at once, for we certainly do not want them.'

Like Marksman, Carnegie had strong anti-French sentiments: 'We do not mind the Frenchman's dogs in moderation; and we countenance Belgian barrels, but the line must be drawn somewhere, and the preservation of red-legs seems a good place for the boundary.'

In his 1932 book *Sporting Days*, shooting writer Eric Parker mentioned an old keeper who was convinced that 'French partridges were baneful and dangerous species, of degraded habits and infectious in their iniquity. They ran, belly to earth, when they should fly; they educated other, nobler flying birds to run; they quarreled with their betters the English partridges, and drove them from their nests, and for all these reasons they were to be destroyed untimely in the egg and as live and mature fowl by every means known to boys, dog and man.'

＊ The French partridge was introduced to England from France in 1673 when Louis XIV presented Charles II with some *perdrix rouges* from the park at the royal hunting lodge of Chambord in the Loire valley. The gift was thanks to the fact that King Charles had a French gamekeeper at the time called Favennes de Mouchant, who helped broker the deal. Further batches of red-legged eggs were introduced to England in the eighteenth century by the Earl of Rochford of St. Osyth Priory in Essex, and the Marquis of Hertford who had estates in Suffolk.

ANOTHER VICTORIAN SHOOTING TALE

A NERVOUS YOUNG MAN was at a shoot on the edge of a mining district in Yorkshire where during the day miners would turn up to bet on how much game each gun would shoot in a drive. Our friend was not shooting well and after three misses a large miner stormed up. The miner informed the gun that he had lost a good deal of money. If the gun did not improve his shooting the miner 'had a moind to give him a hoiding.' The story does not relate how the day ended. But whatever the case, it is the stuff that nightmares are made of.

LIFE AFTER EMTRYL

BIGGEST BLOW TO GAME FARMING IN RECENT YEARS has been the 2003 ban on the drug emtryl. A European Union directive decreed that emtryl was a carcinogen and thus unsafe in the food chain.

Emtryl (chemical name dimetridazole) had been used in UK game rearing for over thirty years in order to prevent the diseases hexamitiasis and trichmoniasis (gapes) in pheasants and partridges. There is no alternative to emtryl except for some herbal compounds which are so far unproven. A drug called Flubenvet is recommended as a poultry wormer but keepers have discovered unofficially that another drug called Panacur, which is intended for livestock, works much better. The problem is that Panacur is licensed only for sheep and cattle and not for birds and is therefore strictly illegal when used on shoots.

Notwithstanding some limited blackmarket supplies which have found their way into Britain from eastern Europe, most shoots have managed reasonably well without emtryl. Gamebirds tend to develop illnesses when they are stressed, and the National Gamekeepers Organisation advises the best prevention of disease is a low stress environment with the best possible diet, a clean water supply and hygienic pens. As to stocking densities, the Game Conservancy Trust advises no more than three hundred birds per acre of release pen, which, incidentally, is a figure that most commercial shoots find totally unrealistic. The GC also suggests locating huts and pens on clean ground, ideally not used within the previous three years.

Other, rather more realistic suggestions from the NGO include:

- Increase your biosecurity. Use detergents and disinfectants/disposable clothing/ gloves/ footdips/changes of footwear, etc. in rearing and releasing areas.
- Ensure water lines are cleaned, sanitized and checked regularly.
- Reduce feed changes to the minimum.
- Are drinkers/feeders off the ground, on wire and regularly disinfected?
- Is there any weakness in your system that freely allows birds to reingest their faeces? This is a major source of disease problems.
- Could you release in better ways? Some shoots are trying trickle release or even rearing within the release areas.
- Will you be buying local poults? Locally sourced poults will have more relevant immunities, be spared the stress of a long journey and can be delivered at a time when the weather is suitable for releasing.

• Are the pens in top condition, providing a varied, quality habitat?
• Is there plenty of sunlight in the pens for poults to dry and warm up? (Sunlight is also an excellent, free disinfectant.)
• Vermin presence and attacks can cause huge stress. Predator control and good quality cover within the pens are therefore very important.

✳ No emtryl? Try onions instead. Chopped raw onion has long been believed to be a cure for gapes. The early nineteenth century field sports buff Colonel George Hanger recommends in his book *To All Sportsmen* that for the first three or four days of feeding you should feed onions to young birds. 'You should chop up some onions, both the white roots and green tops: this will warm their stomachs.'

The fourth century AD Roman agriculturalist Palladius recommended garlic as a cure for pheasants with 'colds in their head' – or in other words gapes. It was thought that the gape worm was affected by the pungent properties of both onion and garlic.

Incidentally, Palladius and experts right through to the middle of the nineteenth century believed in the superstition that water was bad for young pheasants, and that they should not be given any. We now realise that this was immensely cruel but at the time keepers thought that water would give young birds a cold and bring on gapes.

✳ In 1883 the Entomological Society of London published a paper recommending a solution of fifteen grains of salicylate of soda in fifteen hundred grains of distilled water as a cure for gapes in partridges. It was also said that turpentine was effectual if applied by a feather to the bird's windpipe.

RABBITS

The Victorian baronet and naturalist Sir Victor Brooke was the greatest rabbit shot of his generation. On 23 November 1891, at his Irish family seat Colebrook Park, he managed to shoot 740 bunnies in one day. A precise man, Sir Victor fired exactly one thousand cartridges – half from his right shoulder and the other half from his left. With his last shot he changed his mind, spared the rabbit, and shot a woodcock instead.

BILLY'S BOWLER

Strangest sartorial shooting tradition in England are the bowler hats worn by the keepers at the Earl of Leicester's seat, Holkham in Norfolk.

The bowler, a hard felt hat, was created in 1850 by London hatters James Lock for William Coke, a progressive farmer, whose agricultural achievements later earned him an earldom. Also known as the 'Coke' it was a domed hat devised to protect the heads of gamekeepers from branches of trees while they rode on horseback. It was closely fitted to the head so it would not easily fall off. Later on, when they began to shoot vast numbers of pheasants at Holkham, the bowler was useful protection from falling birds…and poachers.

William Coke tested the strength of Lock's first bowler by placing it on the floor of their shop and jumping on it. Since it withstood his weight he bought it for twelve shillings and ordered several more.

Far from remaining headwear for labourers, the bowler became a must for the middle classes. Peaking in popularity towards the end of the nineteenth century it was less formal than the top hat of the upper classes but rather smarter than the soft felt of the lower middles. The name bowler comes from the sub-contractors Thomas and William Bowler, from South London, who made the hats for Lock.

The hat is known in Norfolk as the 'Billy Coke' or 'Billycock.' To this day it is still worn by the eight keepers at Holkham.

COLONEL GEORGE HANGER

One of the finest fellows in shooting history is Colonel George Hanger, bon viveur and sportsman, who is best remembered for his book *To All Sportsmen, Farmers and Gamekeepers.*

Old Etonian Hanger (1751 to 1824), friend of the Prince Regent, had strong views on everything from the care of horses to monogamy which he pronounced was 'contrary to human nature and common sense.' After leaving Eton (where he had spent nightly forays in Windsor while conducting an affair with 'a daughter of a vendor of cabbages'), Hanger began his military career in the army of Frederick the Great. He returned to England and joined the 1st Regiment of Footguards. Long-nosed but considered handsome he was prone to violence and had fought three duels by the age of twenty-one. While a guards officer he married in a Romany ceremony a gypsy, whom he called 'the lovely Egyptea of Norwood.' But life with irascible George was not to her taste and she ran off with a tinker.

On his father's death Hanger became the fourth Baron Coleraine though he bristled if people addressed him by his title.

To All Sportsmen is a rambling collection of advice including everything to do with shooting. Hanger was obsessed in protecting his woods from poachers and used all manner of man traps and spring guns. His favourite device was a six pounder cannon loaded with marbles and clay balls with holes drilled through them. When this lot was fired the clay balls made a 'terrible whizzing noise, and, together with the marbles buzzing about a fellow's ears, would make him think that the very devil was in the wood.' Hanger also suggested that you build your keeper a treehouse 'like a martello tower only in miniature' and mount the cannon on it in order blast the enemy from above. 'I am of opinion if, about two or three times a week, my gamekeeper and self were to fire about three or four rounds each into the wood that the very devil himself would not go into it.'

Hanger became great friends with the Prince Regent, later George IV, and they spent much time whoring and drinking together. The only surviving painting of Hanger was commissioned by the Prince. It remains in the Royal Collection. He died from a convulsive fit aged seventy-three at his London house near Regent's Park.

YAWN

FIRST PRIZE FOR THE DRIEST BOOK on the subject of shooting goes to Oklahoma professors Dr George G. Oberfell and Charles E. Thompson for their 1957 epic *The Mysteries of Shotgun Patterns*. Having carried out many, many tests over many, many years about which they wrote many, many words, they arrived at the conclusion that shot load is more important than shot gauge when it comes to ensuring a clean kill.

DUMB PRICE FOR A DECOY

MYSTERY SURROUNDS THE ORIGINS OF THE WORD DECOY. Some say it comes from the name of the Dutchman called De Koy who invented the original duck decoy back in the early nineteenth century. Others insist that the word came from the Dutch *eeende kooi*, meaning 'duck cage' on the basis that a decoy was originally a small pond with a long cone-shaped wickerwork tunnel, used to catch wild ducks.

Whatever the case, vintage decoys have become highly collectable. January 2007 saw a world record price of $856,000 paid for a carved wood merganser hen decoy made in 1875 by Lothrop Holmes of Kingston, Massachusetts. And two wooden pintails, bought by a Michigan dealer in 1972 for $25 fetched $90,000 in the same sale. Gary Guyette, co-owner of Guyette & Schmidt, a Maryland auction house that specialises in antique decoys, said the serious decoy collectors tend to be very rich men. 'What we've got is a dozen collectors who make hundreds of millions of dollars a year,' Guyette explains. 'If you have a $30,000 decoy and they like it, they might pay $130,000 for it.'

✳ Serious pigeon shots swear that dead birds make the best decoys. You should cut off the eyelids of a dead pigeon in order to convince the birds above that the bird on the ground is dead.

TRIGGER CHENEY

America's most talked about shooting accident of recent years concerns American Vice-President Dick Cheney who wounded his host, millionaire lawyer Harry Whittington during a Texas quail hunt in 2006. Whittington received pellets to the face. 'It looked like he kind of had chicken pox,' his daughter reported. 'He's so lucky. It's a miracle he's alive.'

In Britain we wear tweed while shooting. In Texas they prefer flourescent orange vests. But even this garb, worn by both men, failed to prevent Cheney from whacking his companion in the cheek, neck and chest. Quail are to Texas what grouse are to Scotland. The little birds fly low and fast and guns must never shoot through the line…which is what Cheney did.

Simon Clarke of the British Association for Shooting and Conservation had this advice for Cheney: 'We advise that you should never pull the trigger until you are sure of what you are shooting at. This might usefully be applied to US foreign policy as well.' Likewise, US comedians had a field day. 'We can't get Bin Laden, but we nailed a seventy-eight-year-old attorney,' David Letterman declared on his CBS Late Night Show. However, the joke became less funny when Whittington suffered a minor heart attack. Doctors said a pellet from Cheney's 28-bore had moved and lodged in a part of his heart, causing an atrial fibrillation (a disorder in the heart's rhythm). Though Mr Whittington was apparently fully alert and in good spirits, he was moved back into intensive care where he was monitored for a week before being discharged.

❋ The anti-Cheney camp thoroughly enjoyed this incident, not least because back in 2004 arch hypocrite Cheney used his experience as a hunter to mock a duck hunting foray in Ohio in which Senator John Kerry ended up shooting a goose. 'The senator who gets a grade of 'F' from the National Rifle Association went hunting this morning,' Cheney said, to hoots of laughter. 'I understand he bought a new camouflage jacket for the occasion, which did make me wonder how regularly he does go goose hunting?'

THE GREAT AND THE GAY

Let the great and the gay spend their time as they may,
While from pleasure to pleasure they run;
Well, who cares a jot, I envy them not,
So I have my dog and my gun.

Walter Goodhall, 1820

EXCELLENT IN THE PLEASURE OF HER FLIGHT

THE FIRST SHOOTING BOOK was Gervase Markham's 1621 work *Hunger's Prevention or the Whole Arte of Fowling by Water and Land.*

Markham (1568 to 1637) was an English soldier and horse-breeder who turned to writing poetry and long tracts about country pursuits. Markham favoured the pheasant as the greatest of all game birds. He wrote in *Hunger's Prevention*, 'I will place the pheasant as being indeed a bird of singular beauty, excellent in the pleasure of her flight, and as rare as any bird whatever that flies when she is in the dish and well cooked by a skilfull and ingenious workman.'

In those days of the seventeenth century birds were usually shot on the ground. Shooting flying came much later. Markham declared that you should use as large a bore as the steel of your barrels would take. The perfect sporting gun was a 16-bore and at least six feet long. This would achieve maximum range. Using anything smaller on a pheasant was pointless because 'fowl are of such a fickle and cunning nature that a man shall hardly get within any indifferent or near station or to shoot out of level or distance were to shoot against the wind and scare-crow like only to affright fowl with the loss of labour.'

In literary circles Markham is best known for his 1615 work *The English Huswife, Containing the Inward and Outward Virtues Which Ought to Be in a Complete Woman.* This addresses women of the middle and lower classes, who were expected to take an active part in cookery, and it could be said, albeit in a round about way, that this book was the first work to cover the subject of the shooting lunch…

BIRTH OF WINNIE

A shooting party decided the birth date of Winston Churchill in 1874. His father Randolph was hosting a November shoot at the family home Blenheim Palace in Oxfordshire. Much to the consternation of her nurse, the heavily pregnant Lady Randolph Churchill decided that she would join the guns. While walking over some muddy ground she slipped and fell. A day later she went into labour and Winston was born in the early hours of 30 November.

ABSURD LAW

SHOOTING WRITER GILES CATCHPOLE on the subject of the absurd law whereby you have to have your shotgun certificate on you if you are carrying your gun: 'The more certificates are carted about, the more they are lost…If the bloke in the High Street with the gun case is about to turn over the Post Office, would he really be wearing bungalow check tweed plus-fours, canary yellow stockings and a silly hat?'

EXPERT'S TIP

WHEN YOU WIN THE LOTTERY and buy that grouse moor you've dreamed off make sure that the ground is not all the same height.
In warm weather birds like to get on cooler, high ground.
Also low ground may be fogged out while high ground is in sunshine.
Or the wind may be too strong up high but better lower down.

PHEASANT ORIGINS

THE WORD PHEASANT comes from the river known by the Greeks as the Phasis, which flows through Georgia into the Black Sea. Pheasants were numerous along the banks. These days the river is known as the Rioni.

PICKING-UP

ONE OF THE GREATEST COMPLAINTS heard from guns with dogs is that pickers-up are 'stealing' their birds. Shooting legend Sir Joseph Nickerson explains that this is bad manners. 'If challenged pickers-up will usually claim that the dog ran in but they have nearly always sent it,' he writes in his book *A Shooting Man's Creed*. 'If you are a guest it is wise not to complain, but if you have a dog you are perfectly justified in asking the picker-up behind you to leave a few for yours to pick. A good dog at a peg has waited very patiently for its moment and it is disheartening for it to be sent and to find nothing.'

ANTI AUNTY

IT WILL COME AS NO SURPRISE that the politically correct BBC is resolutely anti-shooting – of any kind. In 2002 Britain won eighteen medals, including three golds, for pistol shooting at the Commonwealth Games (pathetically, competitors had to train in Switzerland following the ban on handguns in the UK). Yet the BBC made not one single broadcast mentioning this heroic achievement.

LACKING GUN APPEAL

DESPITE US PRESIDENTIAL CANDIDATES regularly donning camouflage gear and parading with a shotgun in the woods, the American hunter, one of America's most powerful images, is under pressure as hunting land is lost to urbanisation. In ten years from 2006 hunter numbers fell from fourteen million to twelve-and-a-half million. Everything from busier lives to animal welfare concerns is squeezing the appeal of picking up a gun. Worried state wildlife agencies, who depend on hunting licence income, are trying to reverse the decline by organizing hunting weekends for newcomers to field sports.

NO SENSE

BEST-KNOWN SHOOTING FATALITY of the late eighteenth century was a chap called Lord Barrymore, yet another rowdy friend of the Prince Regent. Barrymore died aged twenty-five after being shot through the eye when he knocked over a loaded gun. The weapon had been leaning against a carriage seat and Barrymore had been using it to take potshots at rabbits out of the window.

The immensely rich Barrymore – nicknamed Cripplegate because of his club foot – was one of the founding members of the Four Horse Club, a group of wild young hoorays who bribed coachmen to allow them to take the reins and drive stagecoach teams at high speeds. The club rules included the clause: 'If any member has more sense than another he be kicked out of the club.'

ANOTHER RABBIT POEM

And the rabbit from his burrow
Slyly slinks along the furrow,
Where the high corn hides his route.
Looking timidly about,

Lest the poacher's lurcher nigh
Track him, with far-watchful eye,
To his haunts 'mid fragrant thyme,
And so bite him, ere his prime,
With sure teeth as tooth of time.

Cornelius Webb, English poet, 1790-1850

FRENCH REVOLT

The most popular shotgun in early nineteenth century France was the 16-bore. This was thanks to a law that this was the maximum size of gun to be carried by civilians. The idea was that if there was a rebellion, the peasantry's weapons would be of inferior size to the larger bore muskets of the army.

AN INORDINATE CRAVING

SUCH WERE THE NUMBERS of politicians abandoning their desks and heading north from London in the autumn of 1846 to shoot grouse that the satirical magazine *Punch* suggested that in order to prevent this 'legislative cholera' caused by a 'an inordinate craving for grouse shooting' the Government should encourage its members to stay at home by fencing in Hampstead Heath and stocking it with 'grouse of all descriptions.'

FORERUNNER OF THE PUMP GUN

ONE OF THE STRANGEST WEAPONS ever made was the four-barrelled shotgun produced by London gun makers Charles Lancaster in 1882. John Walsh, the then editor of *The Field* and a self-confessed gun nut, described it: 'This ingenious invention is constructed on the principle of the ordinary revolver with the difference, that instead of the chambers taking a turn before each discharge, a piston-like hammer rod is made to perform a similar office by the pull of the trigger, its head being brought to bear in turn on the centres of the four barrels.'

DISGUSTING

ACCORDING TO SIR JOSEPH NICKERSON, doyen of twentieth century British shooting, you can spot the slovenly grouse moor gamekeeper a mile off. 'On some moors last year's spent cartridges are still in the butts when the new season starts. That is disgusting and should never be tolerated.' Quite so.

A LIFELONG INTEREST IN BALLISTICS

THERE CAN BE LITTLE BETTER SEND OFF for the shooting man than to have his ashes loaded into cartridges and blasted off by his friends. Which is what happened to vintage gun expert James Booth, who died aged fifty from food poisoning in 2004.

Booth's wife Joanna commissioned Scottish cartridge manufacturer Caledonian to mix his ashes with shot. 'He was loaded into our Caledonian Classic, a 28 gramme load, No. 6 shot with degradable plastic wadding,' said a company spokesman.

Mrs Booth assembled twenty of her late husband's friends and they spent a jolly January on a shoot in Aberdeenshire. A total of 275 cartridges were distributed.

Before the first drive, the shells were blessed by Church of Scotland minister the Rev. Alistair Donald. 'It was a perfectly normal scattering of ashes, a few words and prayers,' said Mr Donald, a man at ease with the occasionally eccentric ways of the countryside. 'After all, James had a lifelong interest in ballistics.'

The bag was seventy partridges, twenty-three pheasants, seven ducks and a fox. Human ashes evidently aid accuracy. Mrs Booth noted, 'One of our friends, a woman who had never shot before, got four partridges with James's marked cartridges.'

PUNT-GUNNING

The first commercial shooting was punt-gunning, which became popular in the early nineteenth century. The early punt-gunners tried to shoot as many birds as possible in order to make a meagre living from selling the meat. Hundreds of craft operated on estuaries around Britain and Ireland. But punt-gunning was a precarious and uncomfortable existence.

The punts were flimsy craft that sat low in the water and were prone to swamping. The guns were more like small cannons mounted directly onto the punts. With bores of up to two inches that could take as much as twenty-eight ounces of lead shot, a single shot could kill a entire flock of waterfowl resting on the water's surface. The recoil could be horrendous, particularly if a gun had been loaded for some time and the shot and wadding had become damp. And woe betide anyone who was tempted to improve accuracy by putting the gun to his shoulder. Many gunners died from collapsed chests caused by the recoil.

Greatest punt-gunner of them all was a Yorkshireman called Snowden Slights who made his living from punt-gunning on the Derwent Ings in the late nineteenth century. They say that once Slights was within thirty-five yards of his target he seldom missed. He once hit twenty-four mallard and twenty wigeon with one shot from a gun that weighed 140 lb with a ten foot barrel. His lapwing record was seventy-five with a single shot.

Fully laden, Slights' boat cleared the water by only six inches. He could lie for hours in his punt, soaked and frequently frozen. He once had to be carried home because his corduroy trousers had frozen stiff. Remarkably, he was still wildfowling at the age of eighty.

While men like Slights made a living from punt-gunning plenty of gentleman took up the sport. But by 1900 flock killing was being regarded as unsporting. There were letters to the papers saying how cruel it was. If you fire one shot into a group of ducks you almost certainly ended up with some of them being only wounded. To get a big enough spread of pellets you needed a long distance meaning that the force of the shot was much less.

Punt-gunning is still legal in Britain though these days there are very few exponents of the art. It is believed there are less than forty punts operating around the British Isles today. No gun manufacturer has produced a punt gun in years. About the only recent law affecting punt-gunners is that the use of outboard motors is forbidden.

PEPPERED OCCASIONALLY

THE 1920s SHOOTING WRITER LESLIE SPRAKE offered invaluable guidance on how to deal with that dangerous gun: 'If, on drawing numbers for places, you find that you are next to a reputed dangerous shot, do not go up to the latter and tell him that your life is not insured. It is far more subtle and tactful to harrow him with a vivid description of all the bad shooting accidents (real and imaginary) that have recently happened. Of course, the reply may be: "Oh, if you shoot a lot, you are certain to be peppered occasionally!"'

THREE WAYS TO COOK A PHEASANT

THREE WAYS TO COOK A PHEASANT, as prepared by the chefs of New York's Waldorf Astoria Hotel in those sybaritic years before the First World War...

Braised Pheasant: Prepare and truss a pheasant as for boiling. Line a stew pan with slices of fat bacon and one or two thick slices of veal, put in the bird, season it well with salt and pepper, add a few sweet herbs, cover it with more slices of bacon and veal, cover the stewpan down perfectly air-tight, and put it in a moderate oven and cook for two hours. When done place it on a hot dish, strain over it some of the gravy that will have run from it while cooking. Garnish with sliced lemons, and serve.

Broiled Pheasant: Cut the bird in four pieces and fry them in lard; when browned all over and half done through, take them from the fire, drain the lard from them, brush over with beaten egg, roll them in a paper of breadcrumbs mixed with salt and cayenne, put them on a hot, well-greased gridiron and broil them for ten minutes over a clear fire.

Roasted Pheasant: Singe and truss the bird and put inside a shallot and a lump of butter; lard the breast close with thin strips of bacon, and tie a thin strip of bacon over the larded part. Roast the bird in a hot oven, basting it often with butter. Five minutes before taking the bird from the oven remove the slice of bacon and brown the larded part. When cooked place the bird on a hot dish, strew over it some crumbs of bread that have been fried brown in butter, and serve it with a sauceboatful each of rich brown gravy and bread sauce.

PLANTED BIRDS

Such is the vast amount of vermin in America that they do not 'put down' birds over there. Which poses a problem when it comes to field trials. The remedy is to 'plant' birds, which are then flushed by the dogs before being shot and retrieved.

Charlie Shoulders of the American Water Spaniel Field Association explains the techniques: 'Planting is simply placing one or more birds within a field of cover done with training exercises or other objectives in mind, including scenting, quartering, ranging, flushing, steadying and retrieving.'

Chukar partridge, quail and pigeons are the easiest to plant. 'You just walk into the field holding them by their legs with their head hanging down, maybe shake their head around a bit and then drop them into cover. This disorients them and they will usually hunker down in the cover and stay put.

'Of the game birds that I have planted the most difficult has been the Rooster Pheasant followed by the Hen. Hens can be dizzied and placed in heavy cover quite successfully, especially in spring when they are in egg production. At other times of the year they probably will have to be thrown in or put to "sleep" and placed into cover. To sleep a bird you simply need to tuck the head under a wing and hold the bird quietly for twenty seconds or so. Another way to sleep a bird is to place it on the ground belly up, cover the head with one hand and pull out on the legs with the other hand, stretching the bird out for a twenty count. You can often see the bird's breathing slow down and relax indicating sleep. Care needs to be taken in both of these methods to prevent breaking the bird's neck or damaging the windpipe.'

Incidentally, at field trials in America the pheasants that are to be 'planted' are carried to the field in a basket borne by a person, usually female, known as a 'shagger.' English field trial judges guesting at American events are frequently startled when a young woman approaches them and announces, 'I'm shagging for you today…'

PEACOCK TONGUES AND PUPPY LEGS

'Although we may be willing to acknowledge ourselves in some respects a gourmet, we do not think that our love of the good things of this world could ever induce us like Apicius (fifth century Roman cookery text) to offer our guests a ragout composed exclusively of the tongues of peacocks and nightingales. Nor would be desire, like Vitellius (first century Roman emperor), to serve up for our brother, no matter how much beloved, a feast composed of two thousand dishes of fish and seven thousand of poultry. Neither is our taste so cultivated or refined as to hanker after the delicate flesh of young asses or the womb of a pregnant sow, as served up on the festive boards of the luxurious Romans, or to relish the leg of a young puppy, as greedily devoured by the curious inhabitants of the Celestial Empire (China); nor is our palate so distorted that we could ever fancy, as some of our friends affect to do, the trial of a roasted woodcock or the contents of a snipe's stomach.

'Nevertheless, if put upon short allowance, we might be glad to partake of any of the above dishes, as well as rattlesnake soup, whale blubber and train oil, without at the same time meriting the ignoble stigma of a glutton, since *necessitas non habet legem*.'

From The American Sportsman, *Elisha Lewis,*
Philadelphia, 1857

SO MANY CATS...

Bumper sticker spotted on a picker-up's car in Shropshire:
'So many cats...so few recipes.'

THE ELDERLY GUN

'THERE IS ONE THING THE OLD SPORTSMAN insists on…namely the finding of a wounded bird. If it is to be found he will succeed. The shooters may get impatient, keepers may fret, the evening darken, and the best drive of the day may be yet to come; but there stands the old sportsman, his coloured handkerchief thrown over a turnip top to mark the spot, and his own perfectly broken retriever ranging in search around him. The dog's master never moves, nor does he allow others to move near him, as he considers, and quite rightly, that so doing interferes with the dog's chances of finding. This habit of the old sporting host causes all his guests to avoid long shots, which may be likely to wound, and also teaches them to "mark" fallen game with accuracy…it is the exception for young shooters to "mark" well what they kill, and it is an art not half enough practised generally.'

From Shooting Field and Covert, *by Sir Ralph Payne-Gallwey, Badminton Library, 1885*

SHOOTING RECORDS

The *Guinness Book of Records* was launched as a result of an argument following a day's shooting. It was November 1951 and Guinness brewery managing director Sir Hugh Beaver was enjoying a day at North Slob in County Wexford, Ireland, when the guns began an argument over which was the fastest game bird in Europe – the golden plover or the grouse. That evening over a glass of whisky Sir Hugh realised it was impossible to confirm in reference books which bird was faster. He thought there must be numerous questions debated nightly in the pubs of Britain and Ireland and realised that a book was needed to settle such arguments. And so the *Guinness Book of Records* was born…